FLOWER DREAMS

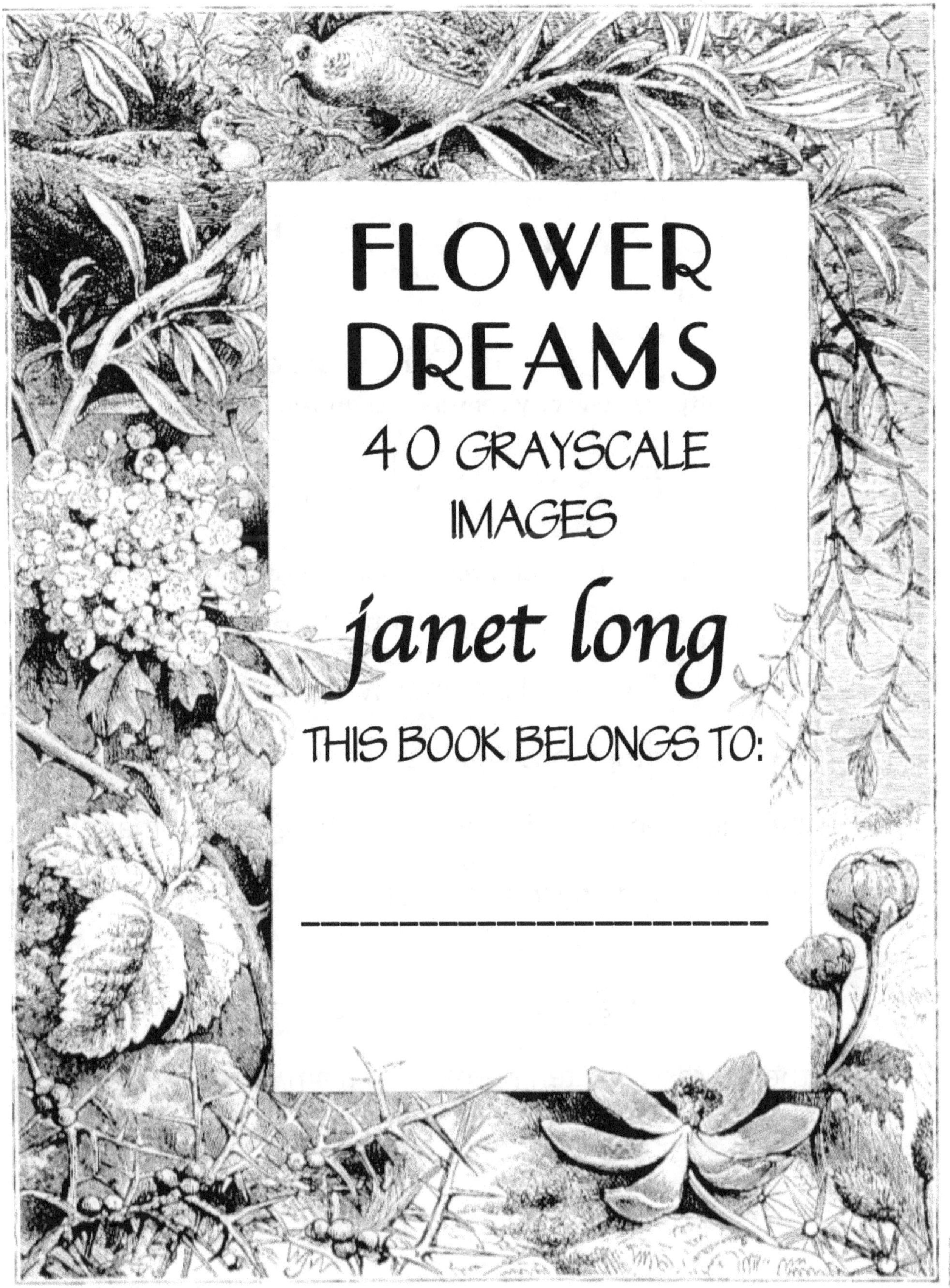

40 GRAYSCALE IMAGES

janet long

THIS BOOK BELONGS TO:

_____

AMAZON AUTHOR PAGE:

https://www.amazon.com/author/janetlong

ETSY VINTAGE SHOP

"Go green! Buy vintage!"
https://www.etsy.com/il-en/shop/AdoptionsLtd

ETSY "JLA" SHOP

https://www.etsy.com/shop/JanetLongArts

[Photography & Watercolor prints, Hand Knits]

This book was developed by Janet W. Long in February 2017.

The images are photographs I have taken in my own yard & garden.

I've included some images from the public domain.

[Contact me if you find any images that are NOT in the public domain. unrise@hotmail.com]

These images may not be replicated in any way without

the express, written permission from Janet W. Long.

ISBN-13: 978-1544035697   ISBN-10: 1544035691

FLOWER DREAMS
40 GRAYSCALE IMAGES

INTRO...

I've chosen some of my own photography from my own yard & garden for this book. I added a few public domain images for you to turn into home décor if you wish. Several of my images in this book are in the 'film noir' style, deep black & white. When coloring these images, I like to leave the blacks intact, NOT try to cover in ink, but use them as a counterpoint, coloring the lighter areas for a dramatic, eye-catching look. Coloring only a small portion can create great drama especially if you use a bright color.

In grayscale coloring, the shading is already there. **Everyone can be an artist!** Just apply a layer of color & there's your picture! I have intentionally put some lighter grayscale images in this & my other books, so you can have a bit more artistic 'freedom' to add your ideas.

Use the blank pages at the back of the book for your notes & coloring implement testing. Discover how your various pencils or crayons interact to create the colors you love. You don't have to buy all the coloring tools & colors out there. You'll see that even if you have only **one** red pencil, you can create many shades of red by using a blue, orange, purple underlay/overlay. Use as many layers as you wish. **You're the colorist!**

If you choose gel pens, felt tips, or other more 'liquid' mediums, please put a piece of cardstock or other paper behind your color work to catch any possible bleed through. You may want to cut out the pages to get a more open space to color. Go ahead, frame your work! Put it on your walls or give as a gift. It's **ART!!**

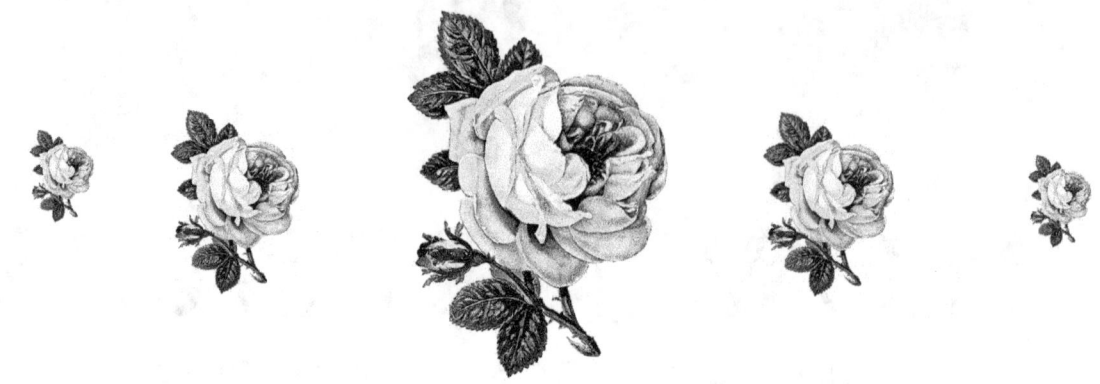

FIND ME
        AMAZON AUTHOR PAGE: http://amzn.to/2g7qeAZ
ETSY VINTAGE SHOP: https://www.etsy.com/shop/AdoptionsLtd
    ETSY SHOP, "JLA" https://www.janetlongarts/shop/Etsy.com

ETSY "JLA" RETAIL SHOP ON FACEBOOK:
        https://www.facebook.com/Janet-Long-Arts-
        192517394097105/
ETSY VINTAGE RETAIL SHOP on FACEBOOK: http://bit.ly/2iS45YC
        TWITTER: https://twitter.com/jan43q
    PINTEREST: http://pinterest.com/janetlongarts/
        LINKEDIN: ttp://www.linkedin.com/profile/view?...

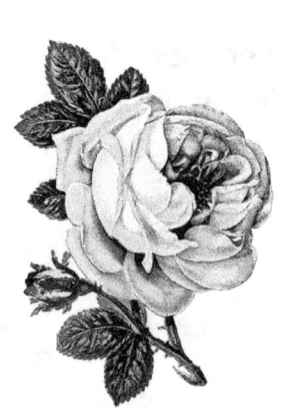

4

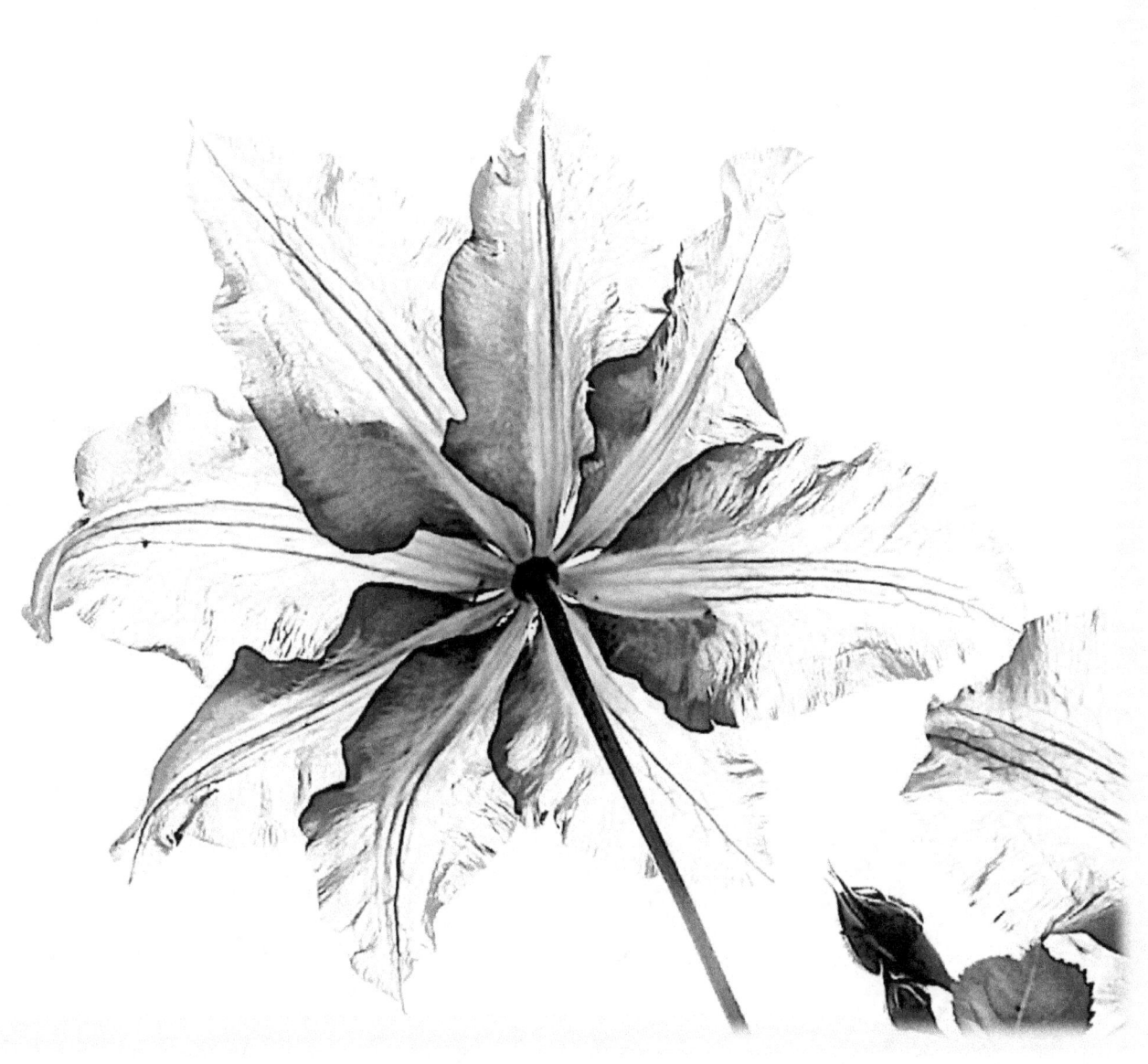

CLEMATIS

CLEMATIS

AMAZON AUTHOR PAGE: www.amazon.com/author/janetlong
ETSY SHOP, "JLA" www.janetlongarts/shop/Etsy.com
ETSY VINTAGE SHOP: www.etsy.com/shop/AdoptionsLtd

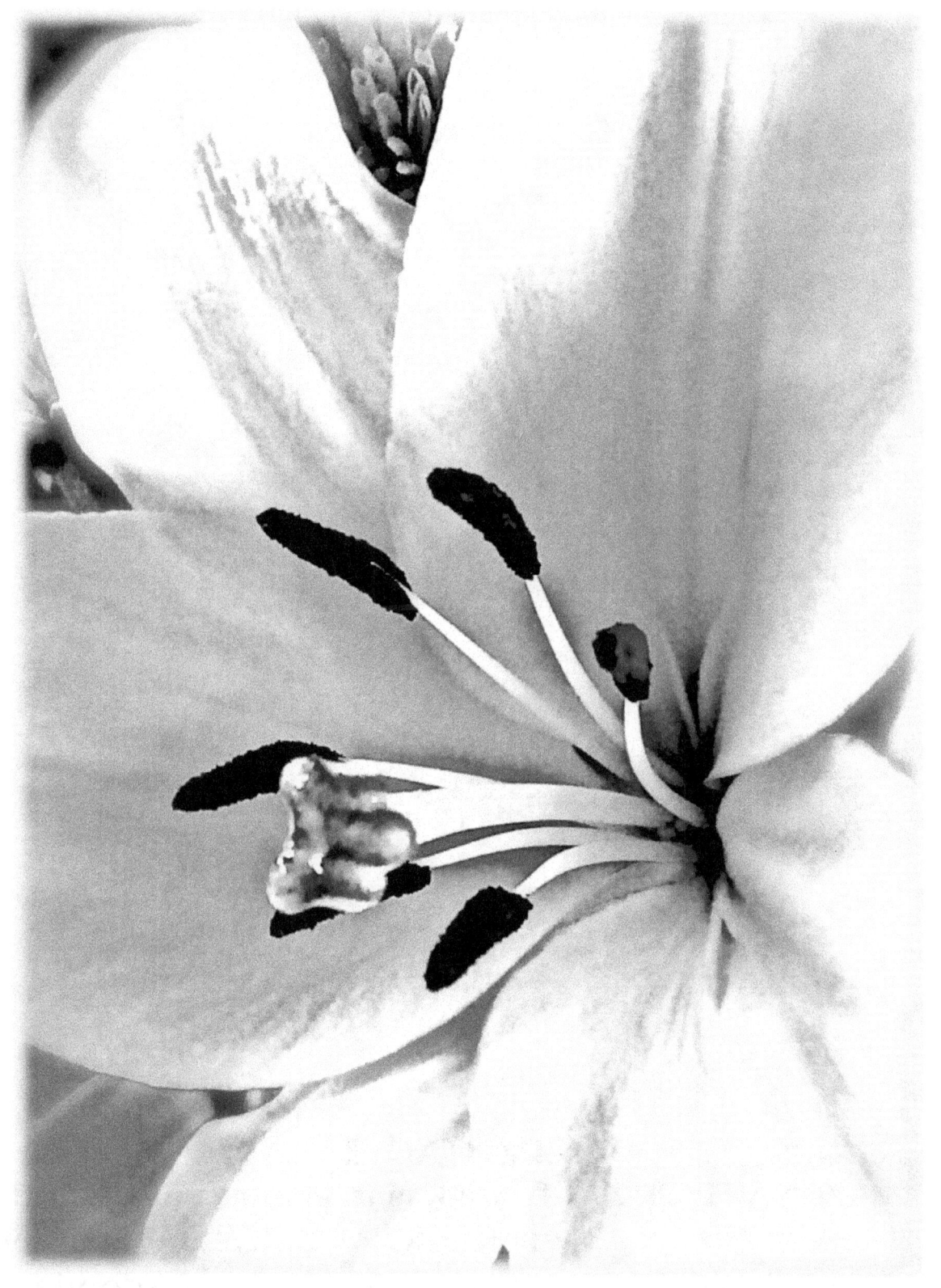

ORIENTAL LILY
AMAZON AUTHOR PAGE: www.amazon.com/author/janetlong
ETSY SHOP, "JLA" www.janetlongarts/shop/Etsy.com
ETSY VINTAGE SHOP: www.etsy.com/shop/AdoptionsLtd

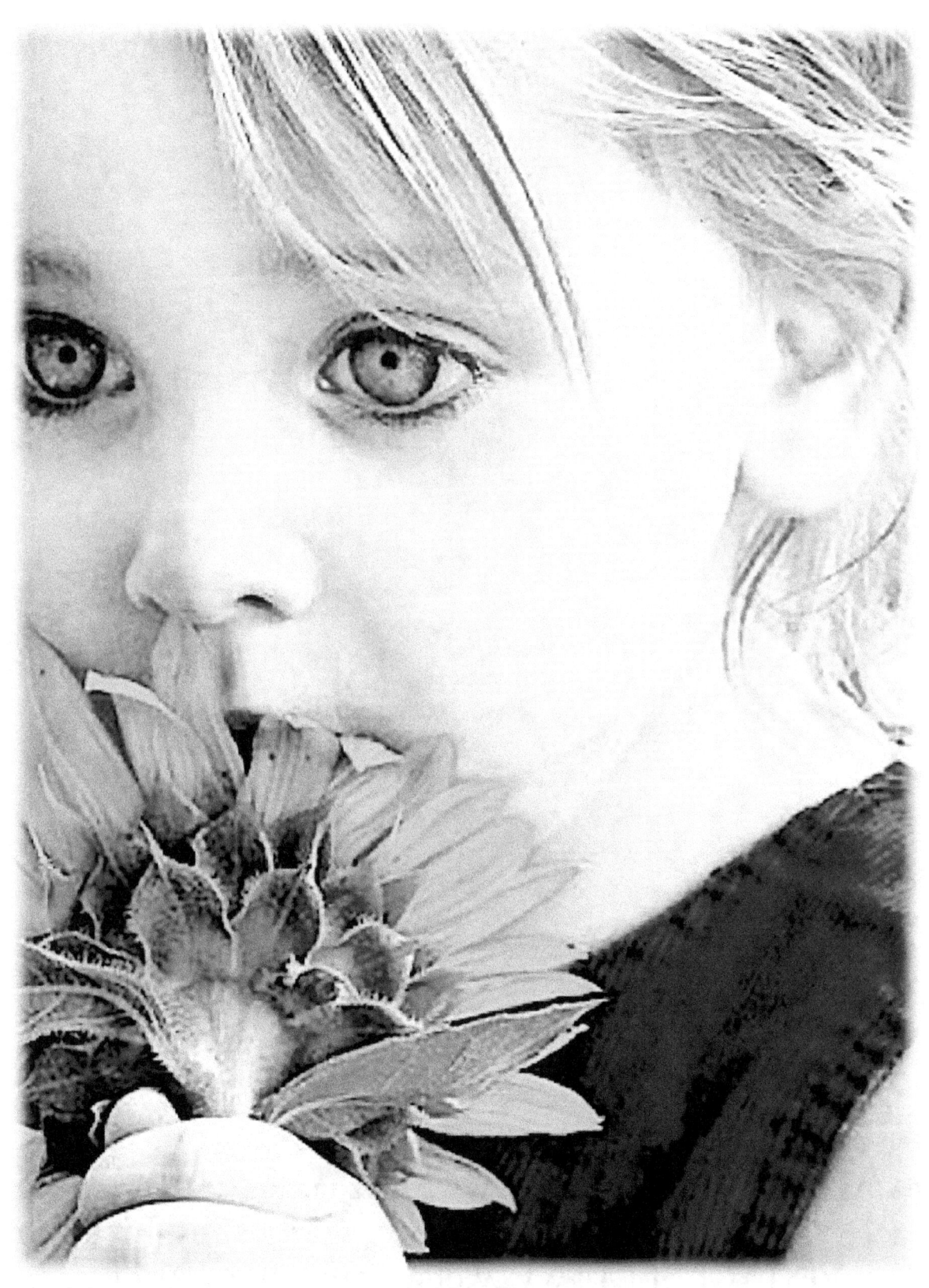

SUNFLOWER

SUNFLOWER

AMAZON AUTHOR PAGE: www.amazon.com/author/janetlong
ETSY SHOP, "JLA" www.janetlongarts/shop/Etsy.com
ETSY VINTAGE SHOP: www.etsy.com/shop/AdoptionsLtd

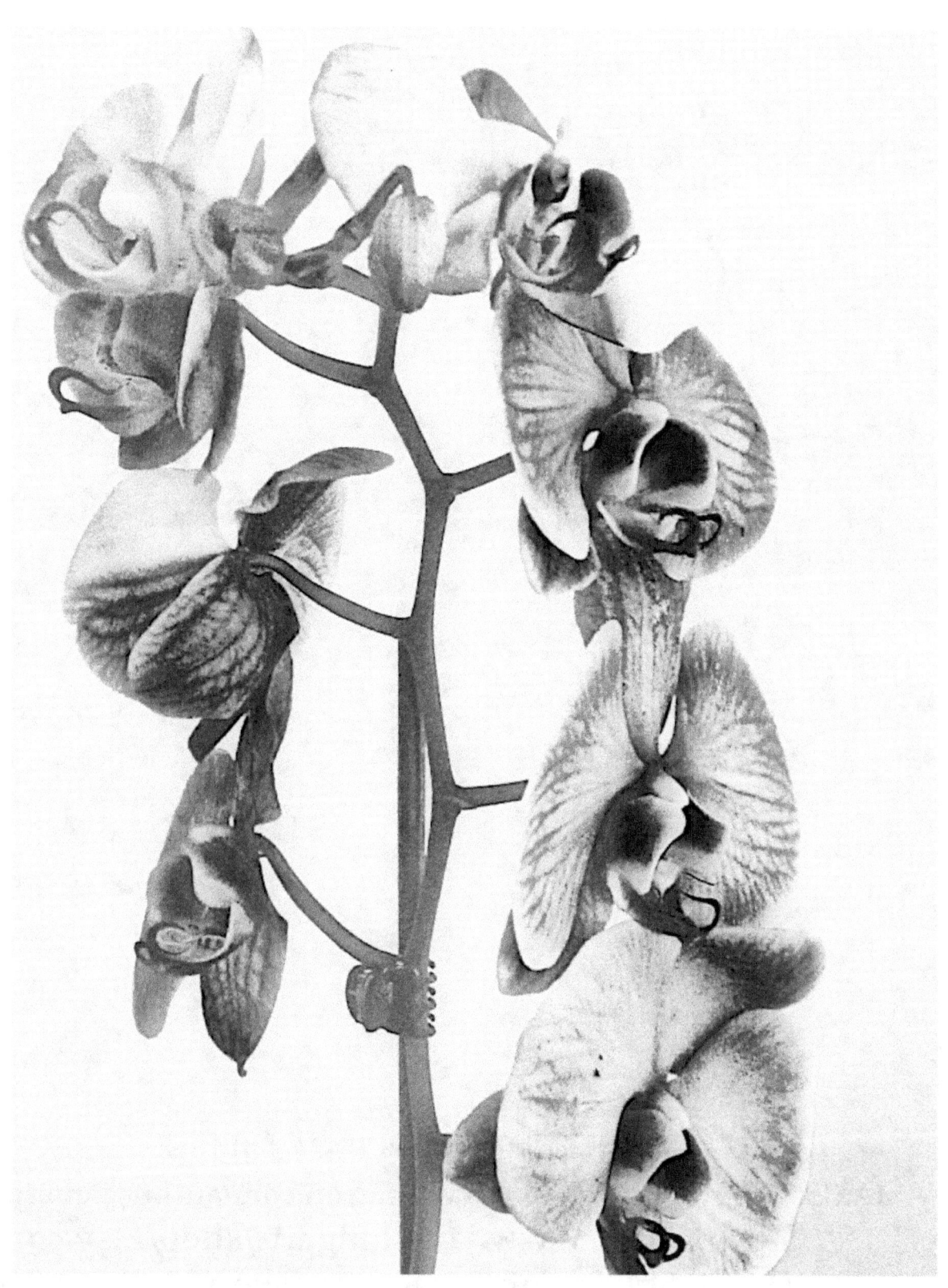

PHALAENOPISIS ORCHID

PHALAENOPISIS ORCHID
AMAZON AUTHOR PAGE: www.amazon.com/author/janetlong
ETSY SHOP, "JLA" www.janetlongarts/shop/Etsy.com
ETSY VINTAGE SHOP: www.etsy.com/shop/AdoptionsLtd

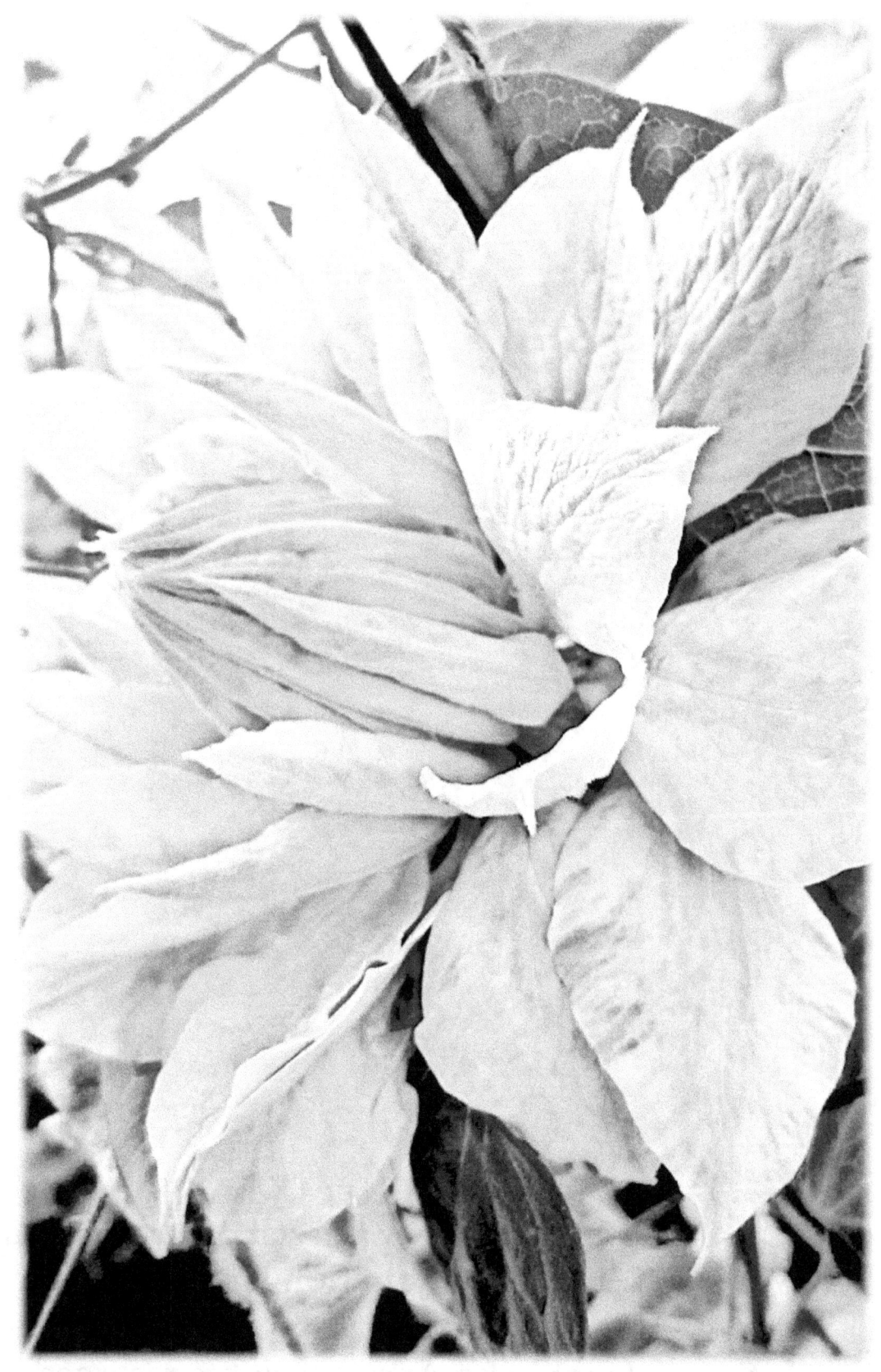

"PASTEL DREAM" CLEMATIS "

CLEMATIS PASTEL DREAMS

AMAZON AUTHOR PAGE: www.amazon.com/author/janetlong
ETSY SHOP, "JLA" www.janetlongarts/shop/Etsy.com
ETSY VINTAGE SHOP: www.etsy.com/shop/ AdoptionsLtd

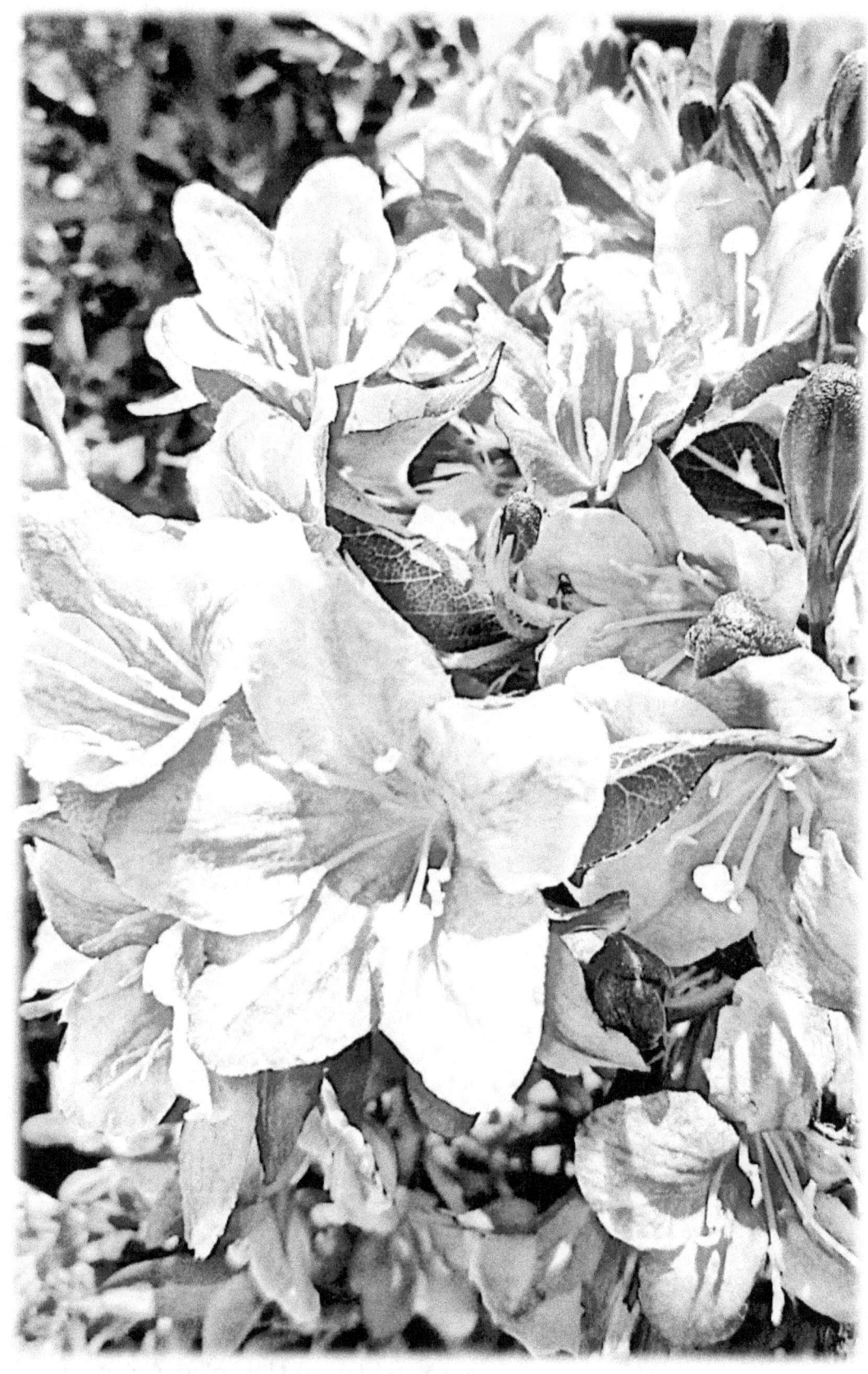

GERANIUM

PINK GERANIUM

AMAZON AUTHOR PAGE: www.amazon.com/author/janetlong
ETSY SHOP, "JLA" www.janetlongarts/shop/Etsy.com
ETSY VINTAGE SHOP: www.etsy.com/shop/AdoptionsLtd

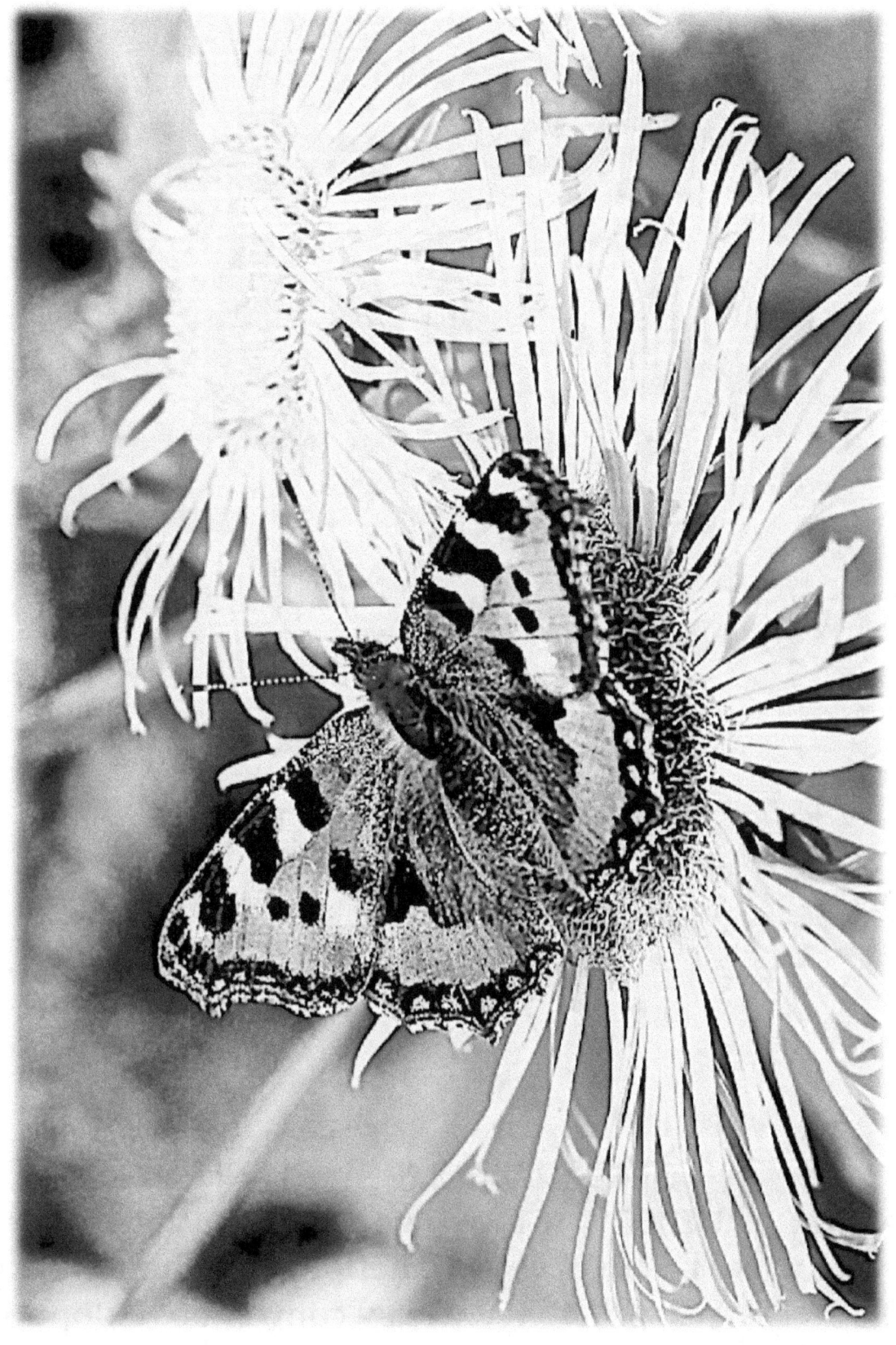

SPIDER MUM & BUTTERFLY

SPIDER MUM & BUTTERFLY
AMAZON AUTHOR PAGE: www.amazon.com/author/janetlong
ETSY SHOP, "JLA" www.janetlongarts/shop/Etsy.com
ETSY VINTAGE SHOP: www.etsy.com/shop/AdoptionsLtd

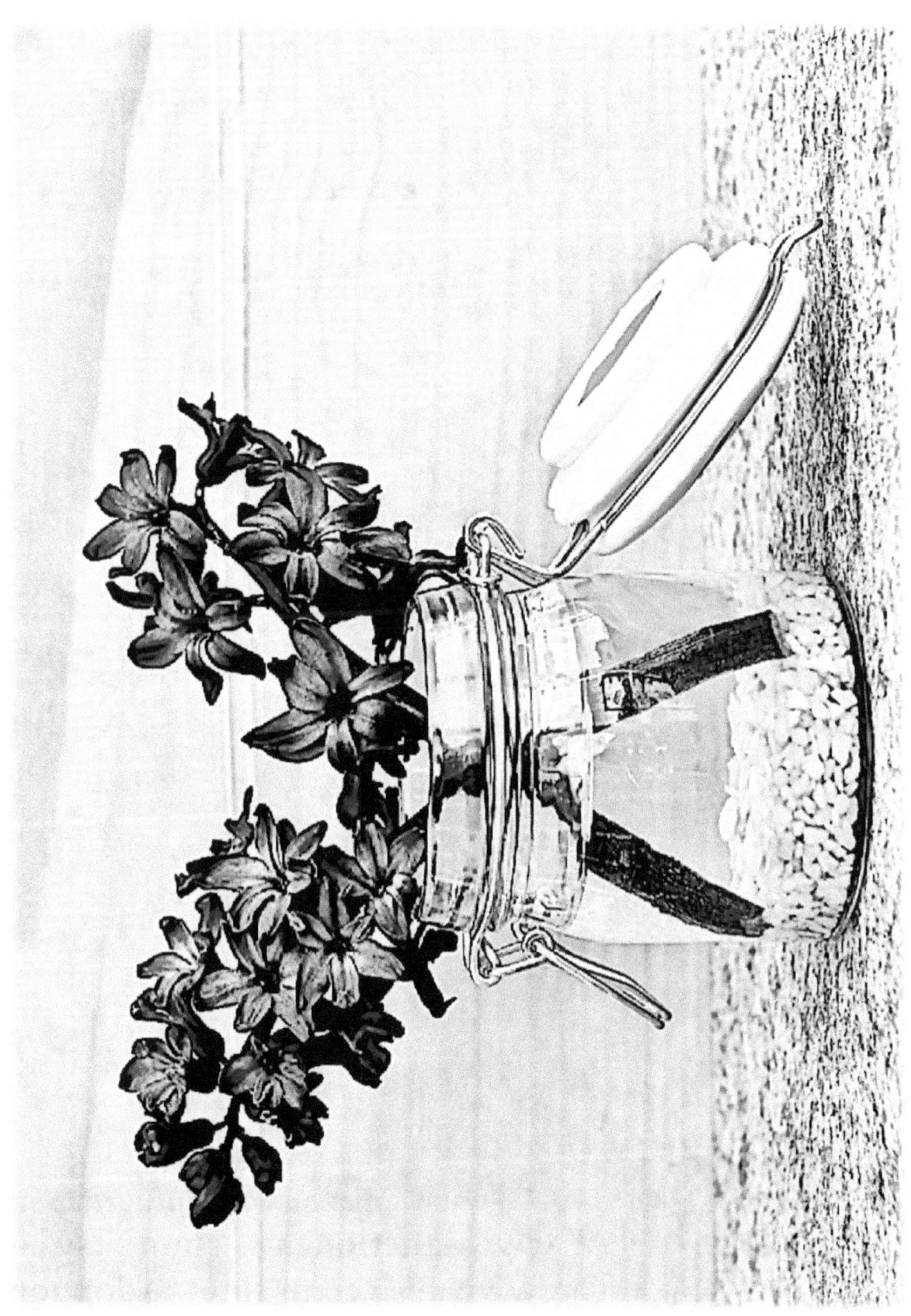

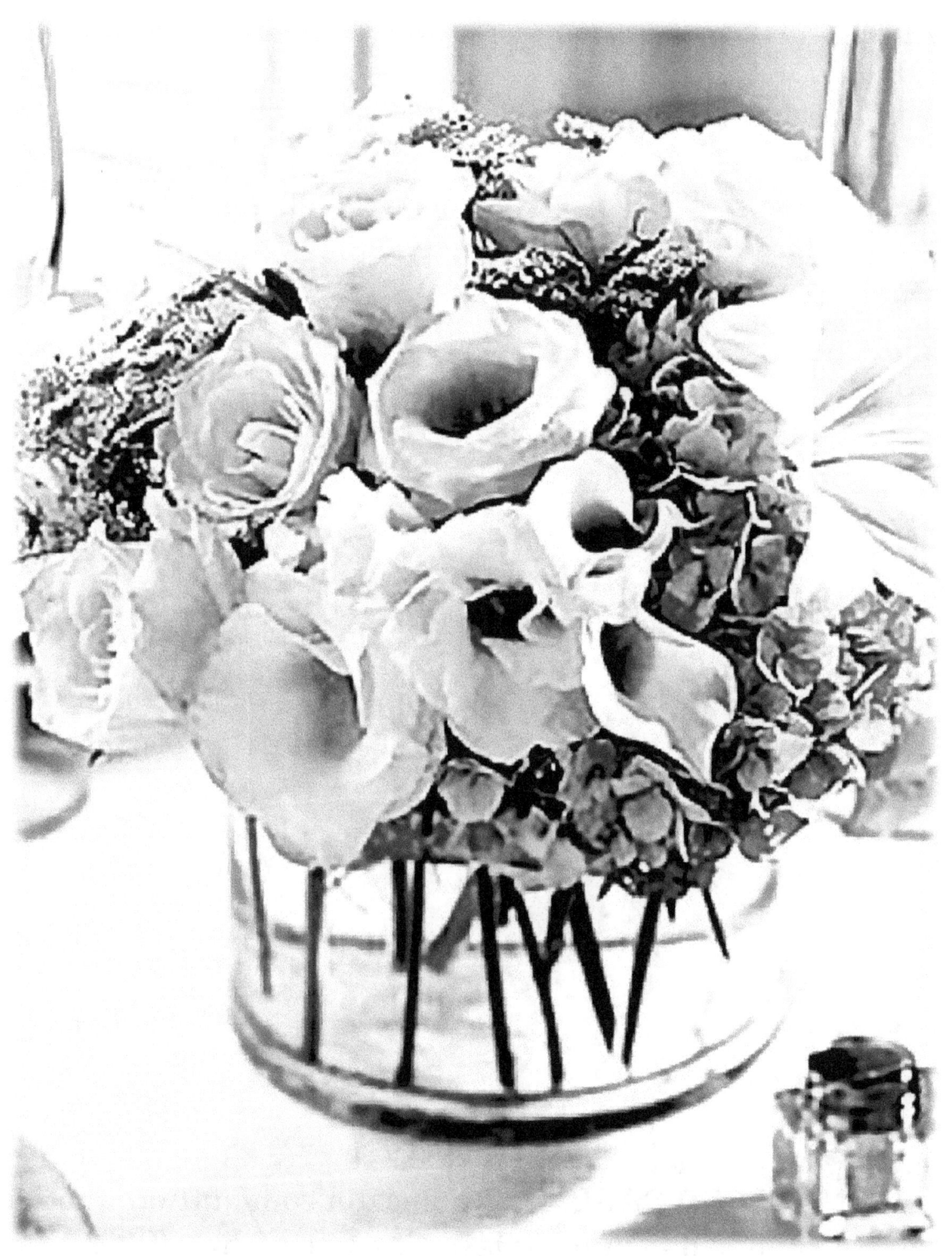

CENTERPIECE

CENTERPIECE
AMAZON AUTHOR PAGE: www.amazon.com/author/janetlong
ETSY SHOP, "JLA" www.janetlongarts/shop/Etsy.com
ETSY VINTAGE SHOP: www.etsy.com/shop/AdoptionsLtd

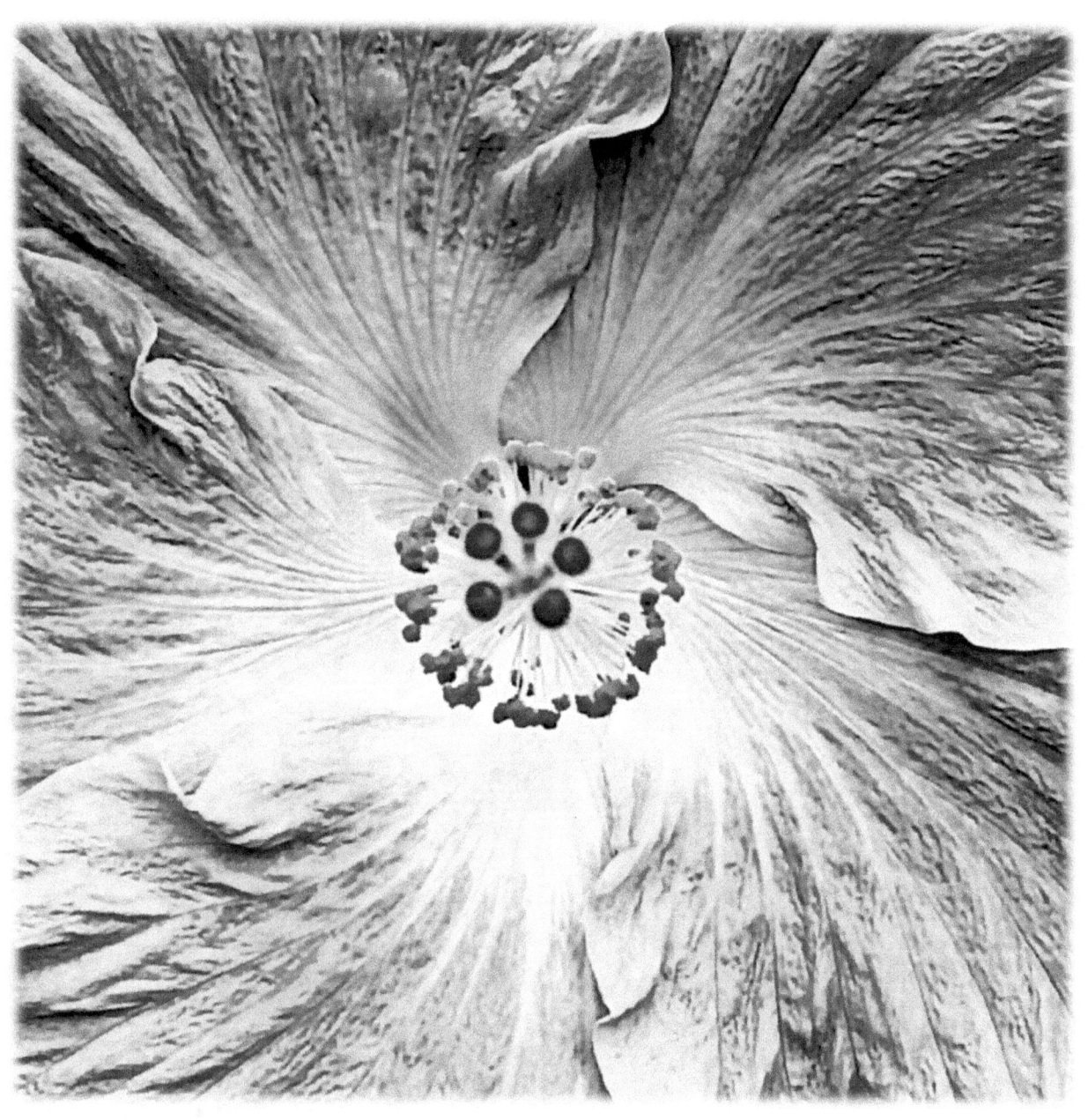

COSY REFUFIUM ORANGE BLOSSOM

COSY REFUFIUM ORANGE BLOSSOM
AMAZON AUTHOR PAGE: www.amazon.com/author/janetlong
ETSY SHOP, "JLA" www.janetlongarts/shop/Etsy.com
ETSY VINTAGE SHOP: www.etsy.com/shop/AdoptionsLtd

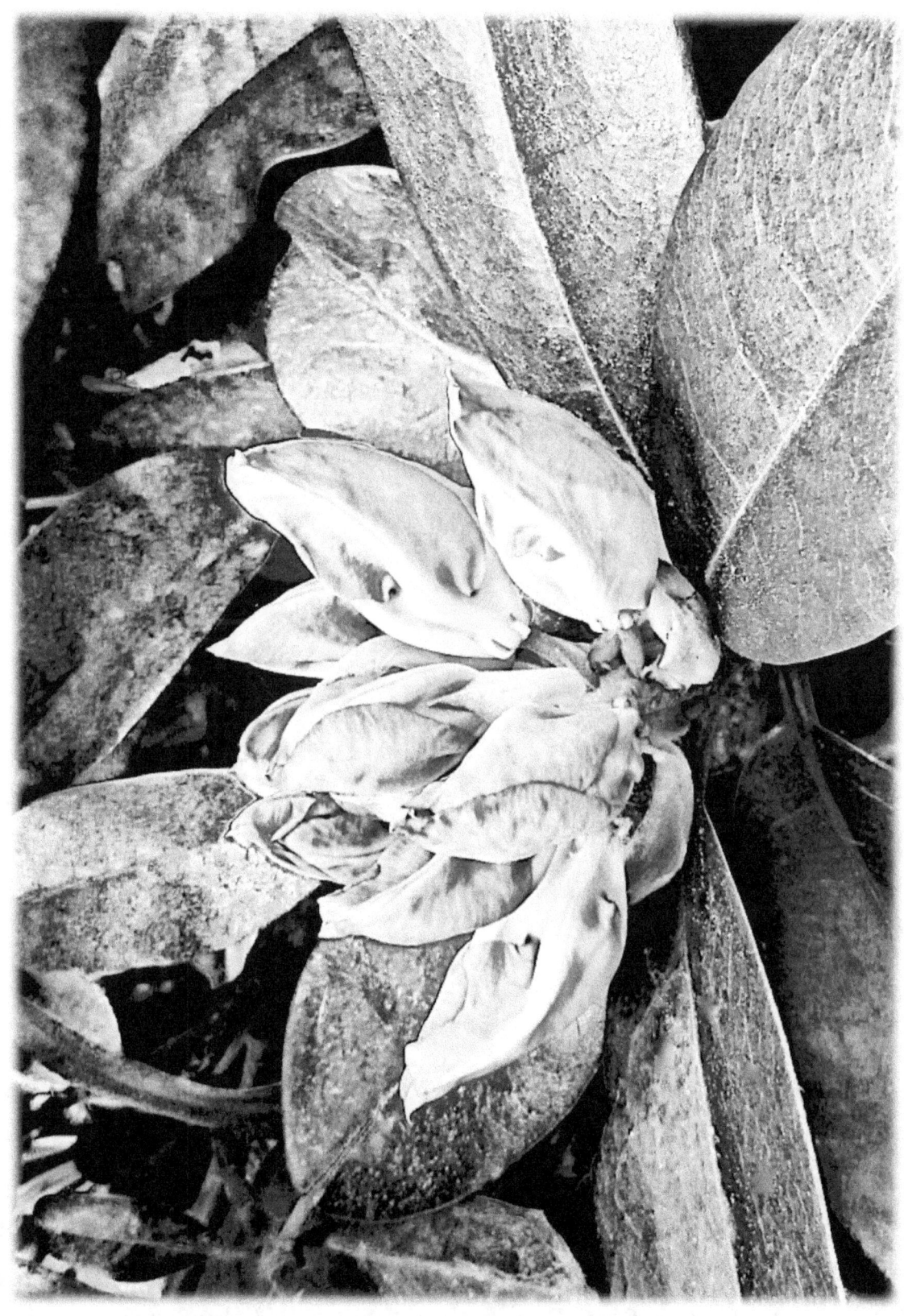

RHODODENDRON
AMAZON AUTHOR PAGE: www.amazon.com/author/janetlong
ETSY SHOP, "JLA" www.janetlongarts/shop/Etsy.com
ETSY VINTAGE SHOP: www.etsy.com/shop/AdoptionsLtd

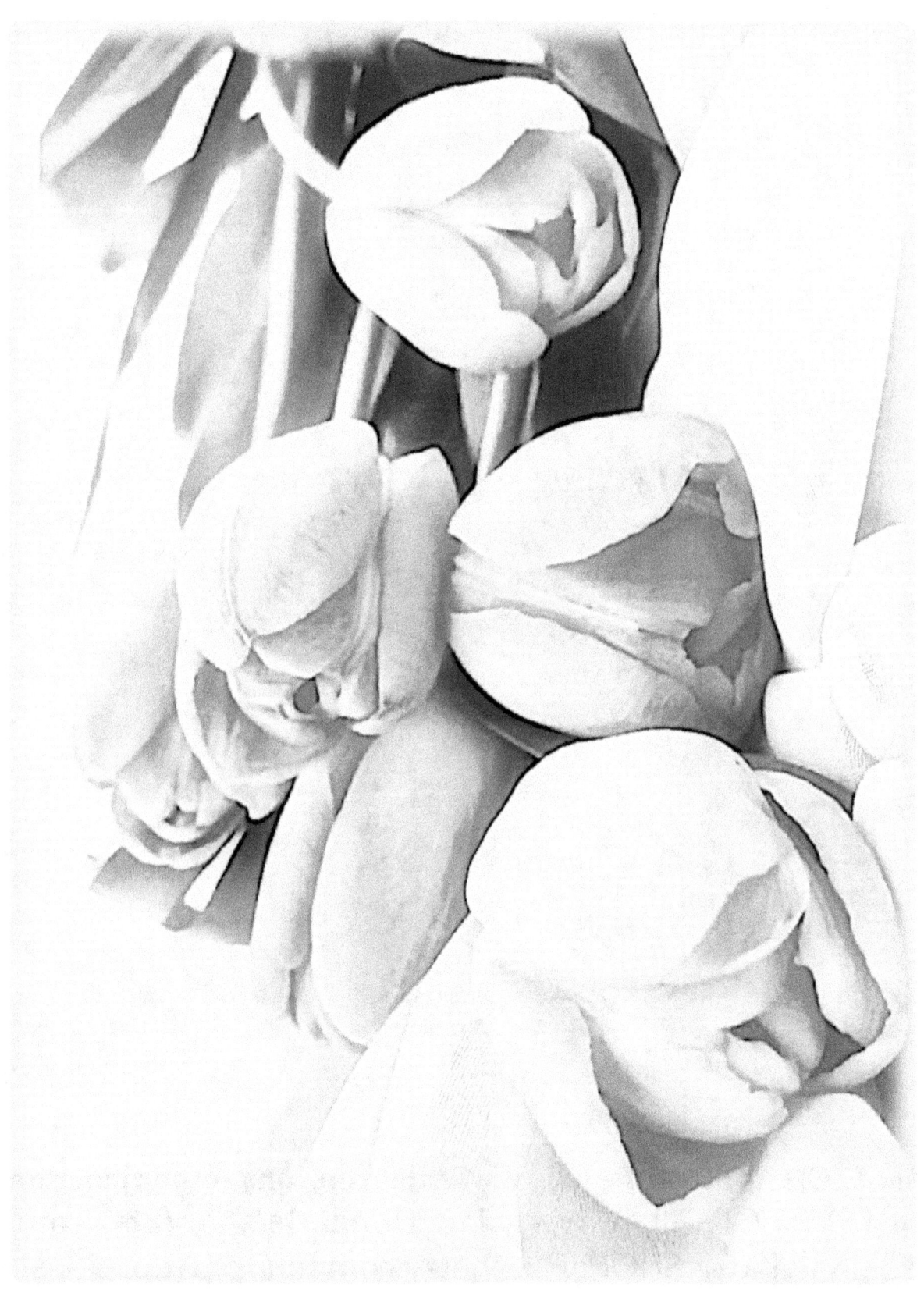

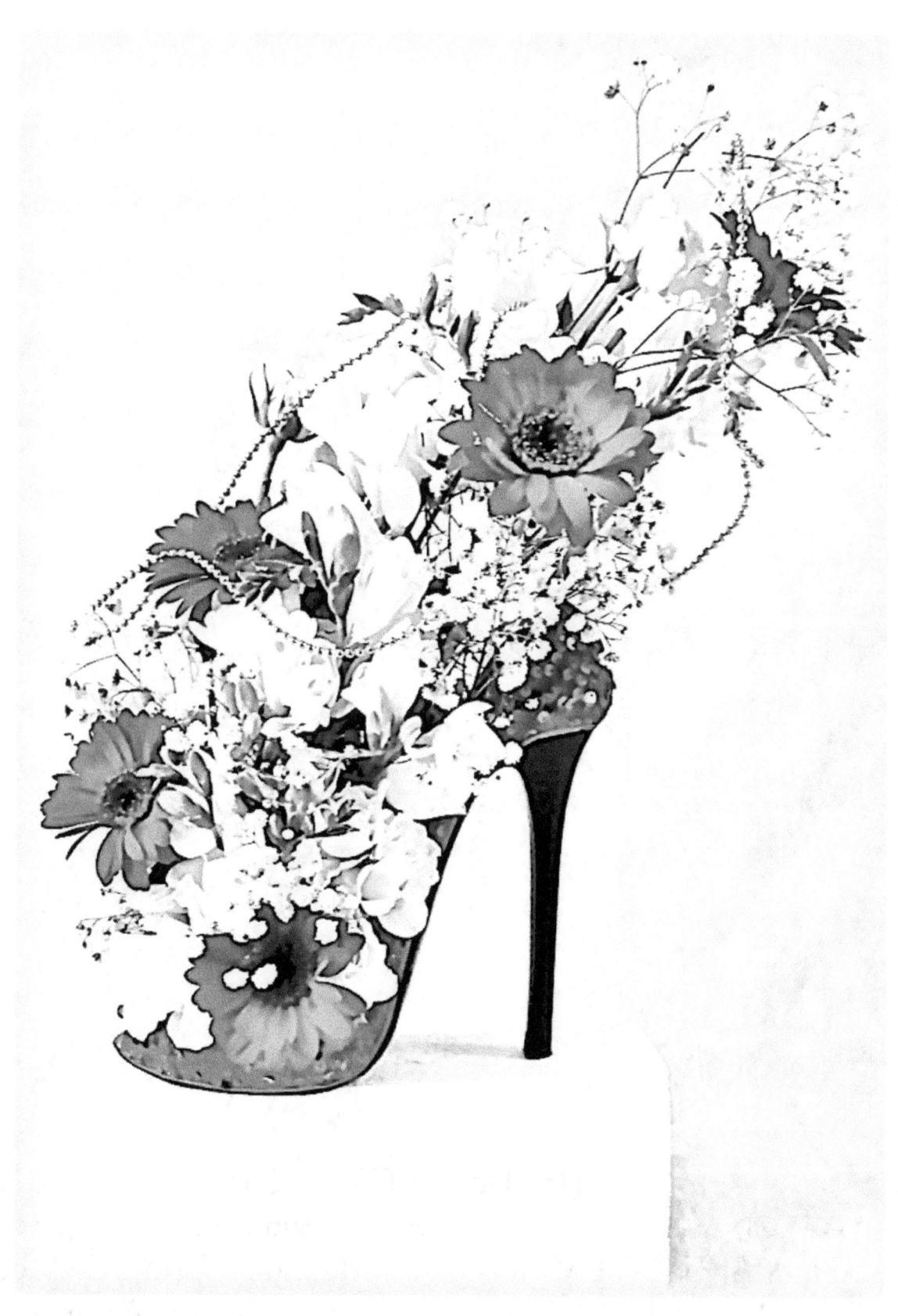

THE PERFECT SHOE!

THE PERFECT SHOE!
AMAZON AUTHOR PAGE: www.amazon.com/author/janetlong
ETSY SHOP, "JLA" www.janetlongarts/shop/Etsy.com
ETSY VINTAGE SHOP: www.etsy.com/shop/AdoptionsLtd

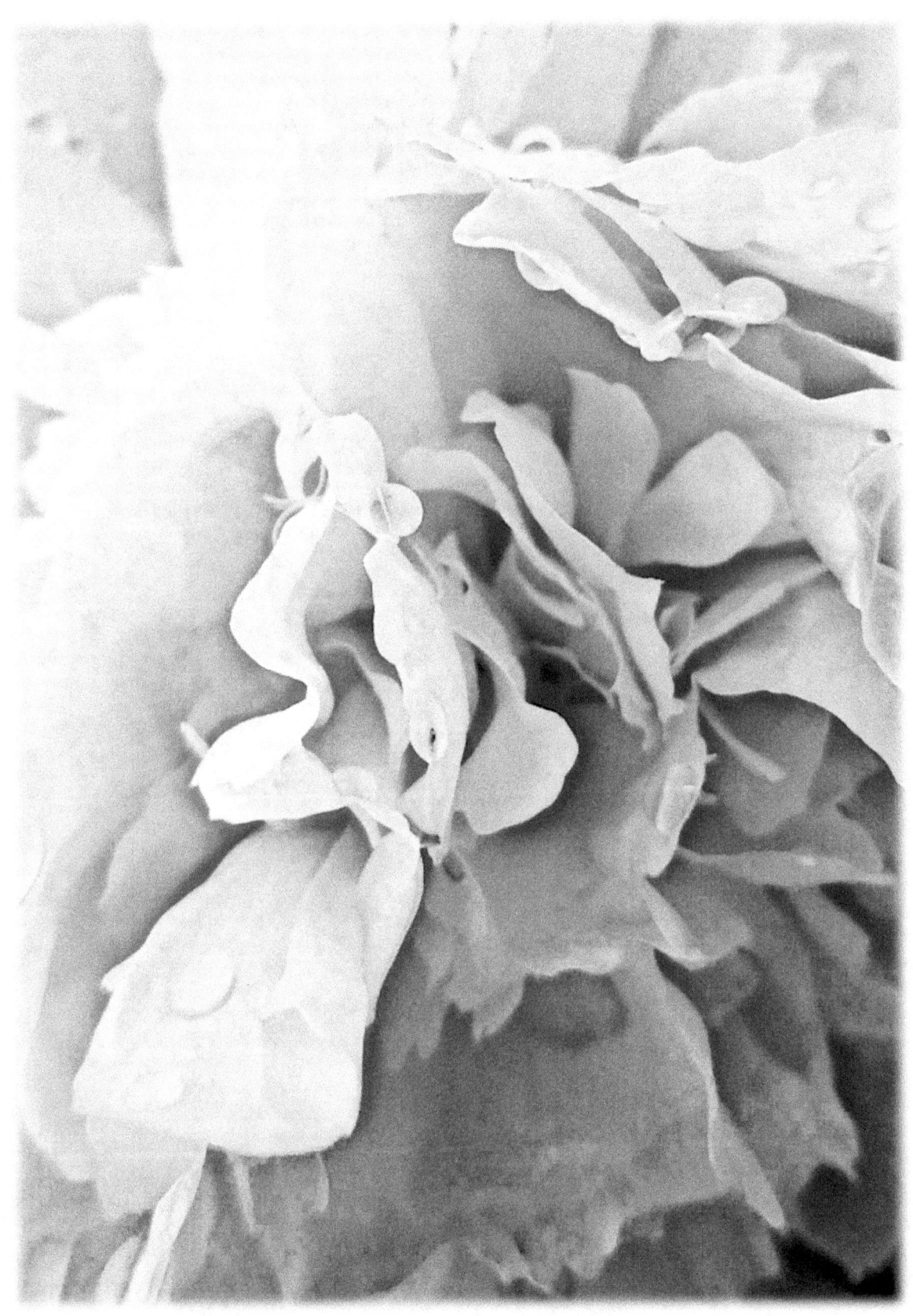

ROSE
AMAZON AUTHOR PAGE: www.amazon.com/author/janetlong
ETSY SHOP, "JLA" www.janetlongarts/shop/Etsy.com
ETSY VINTAGE SHOP: www.etsy.com/shop/ AdoptionsLtd

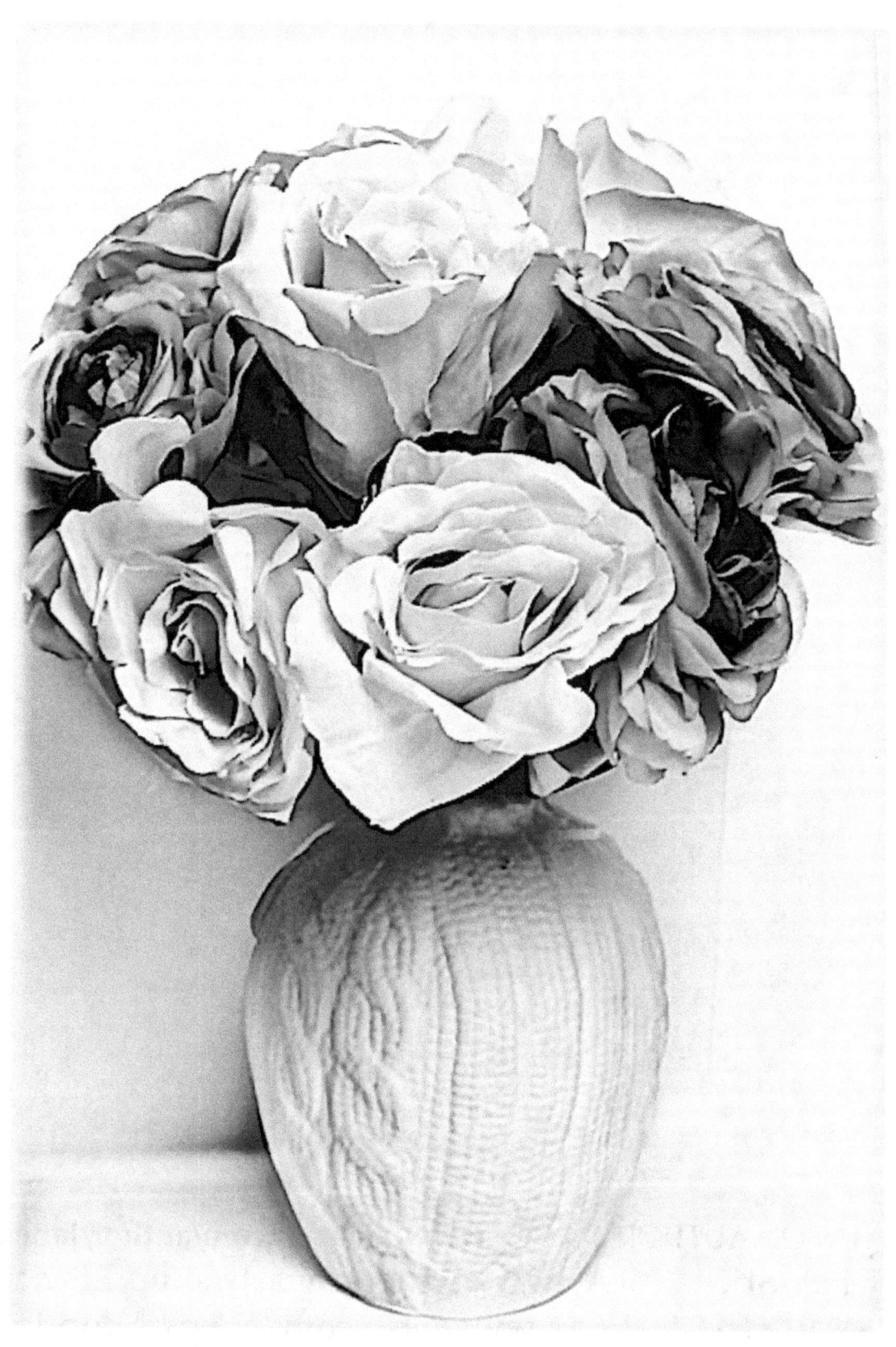

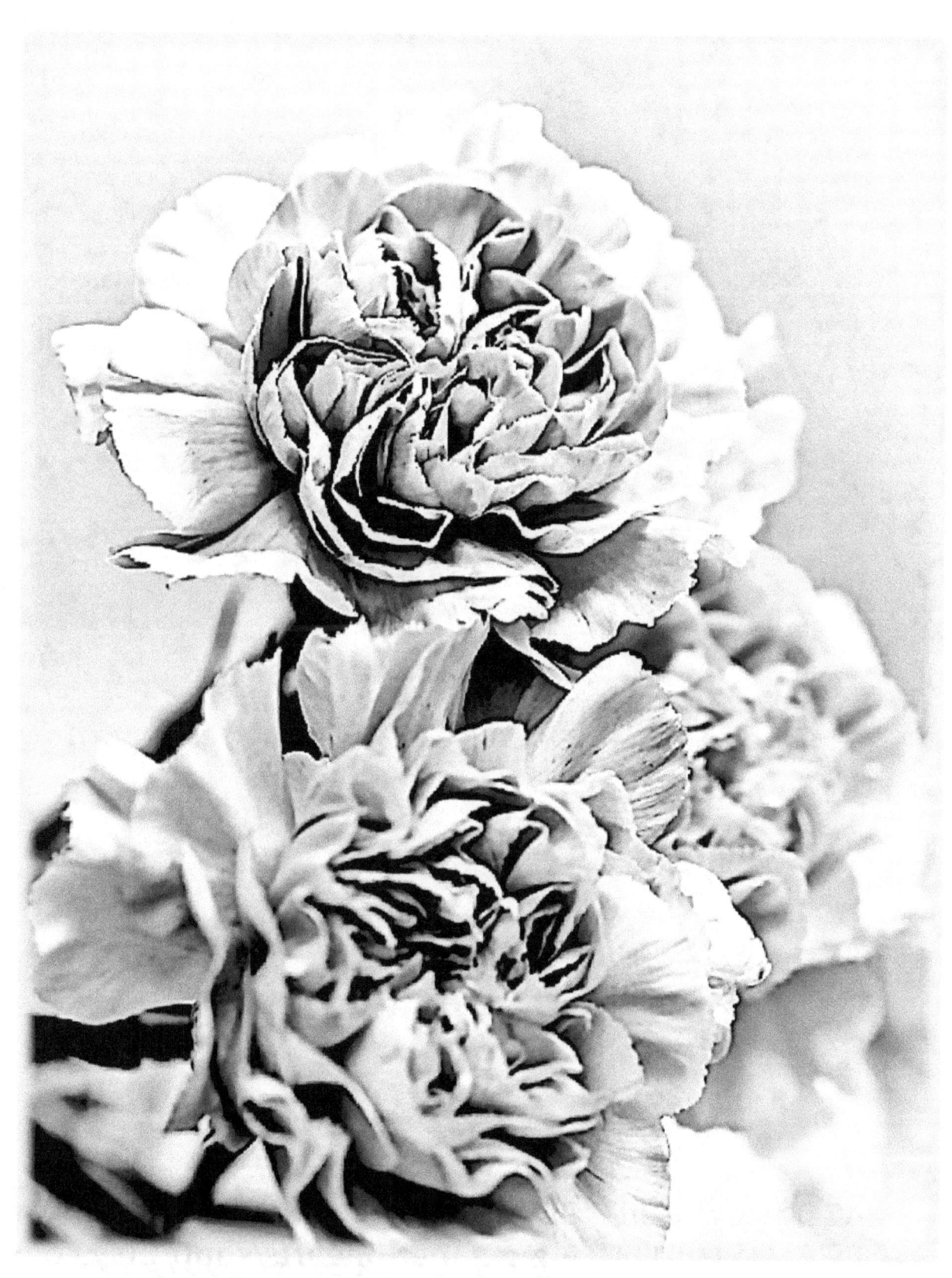

CABBAGE ROSES

CABBAGE ROSES
AMAZON AUTHOR PAGE: www.amazon.com/author/janetlong
ETSY SHOP, "JLA" www.janetlongarts/shop/Etsy.com
ETSY VINTAGE SHOP: www.etsy.com/shop/AdoptionsLtd

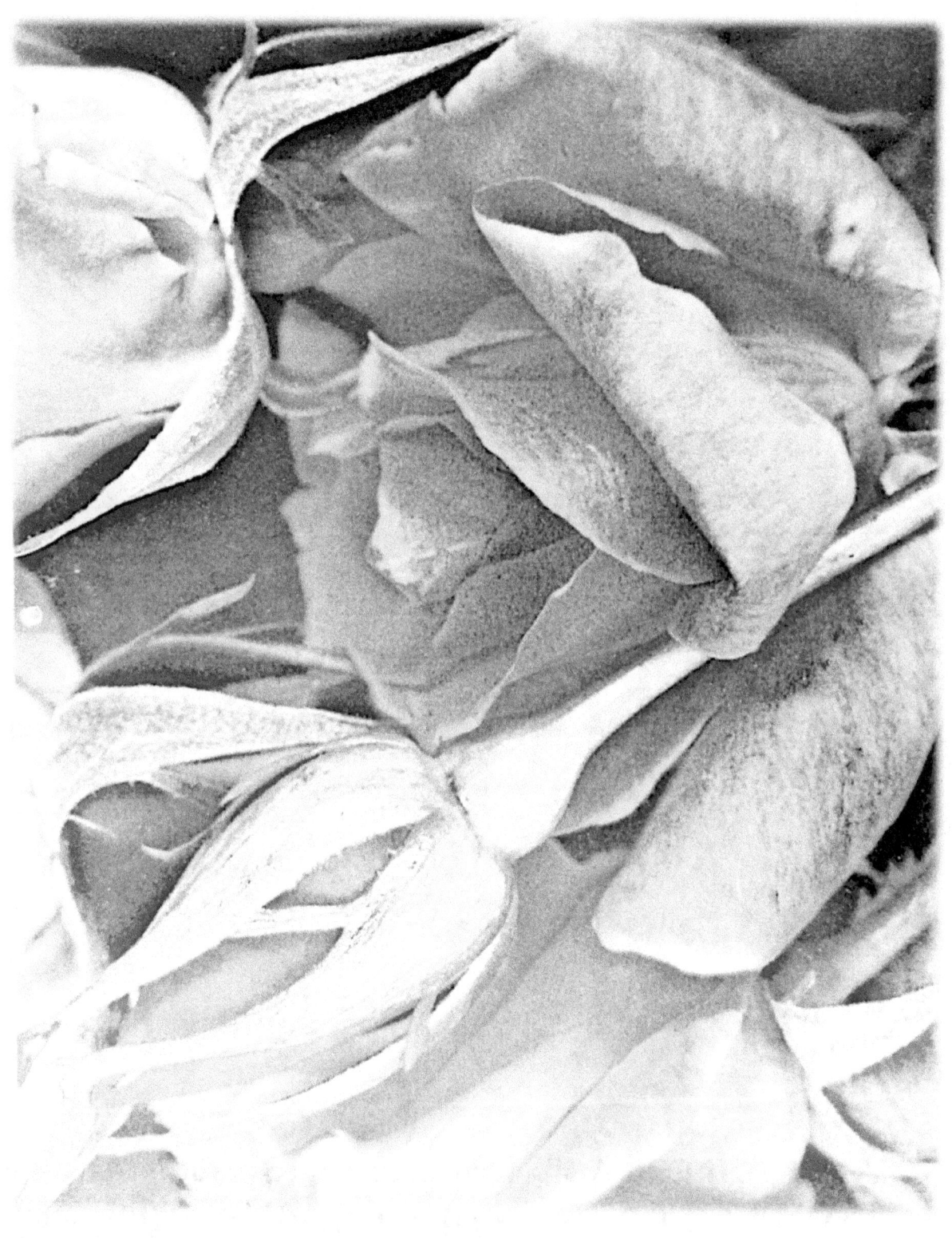

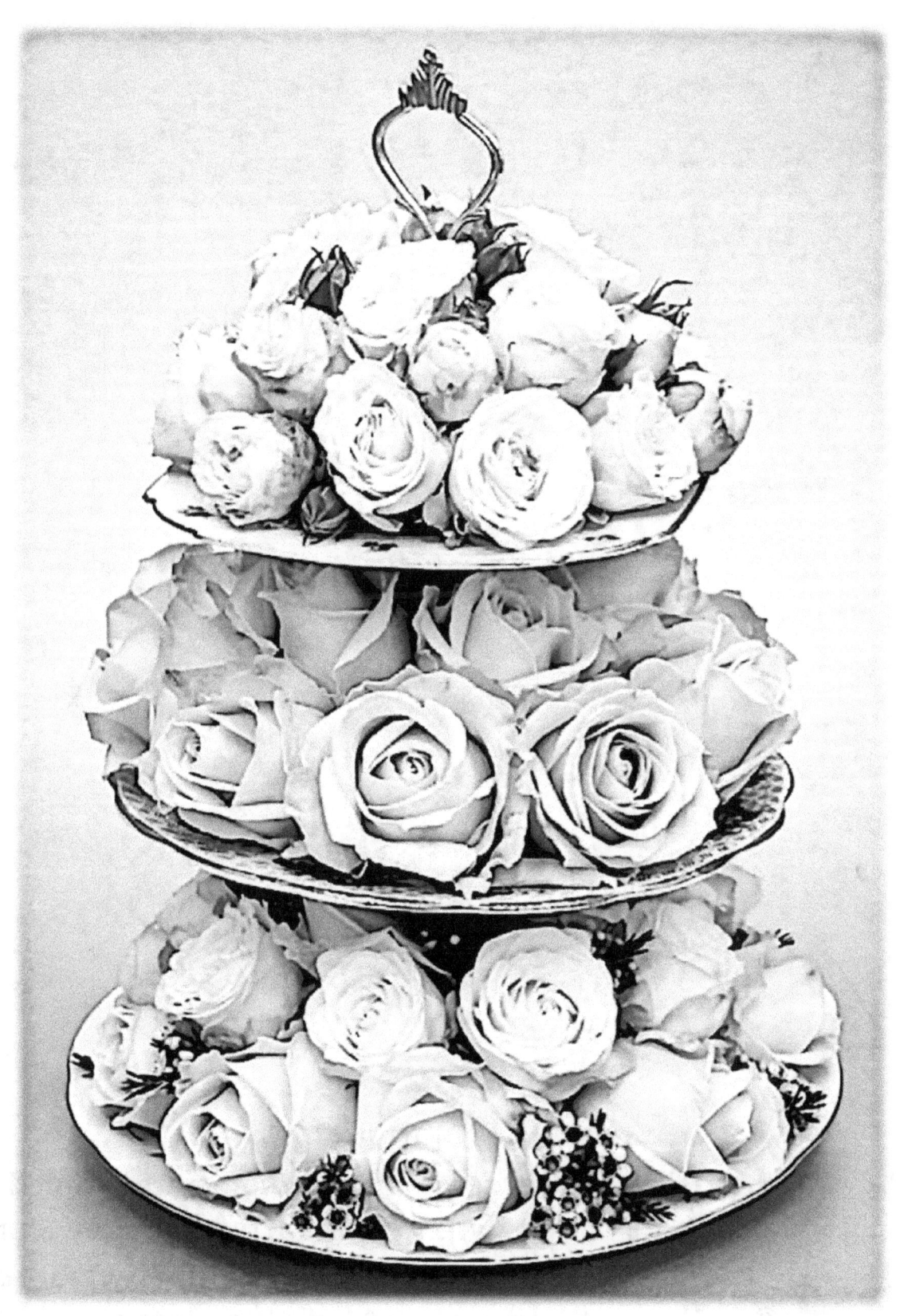

WEDDING?

WEDDING?

AMAZON AUTHOR PAGE: www.amazon.com/author/janetlong
ETSY SHOP, "JLA" www.janetlongarts/shop/Etsy.com
ETSY VINTAGE SHOP: www.etsy.com/shop/AdoptionsLtd

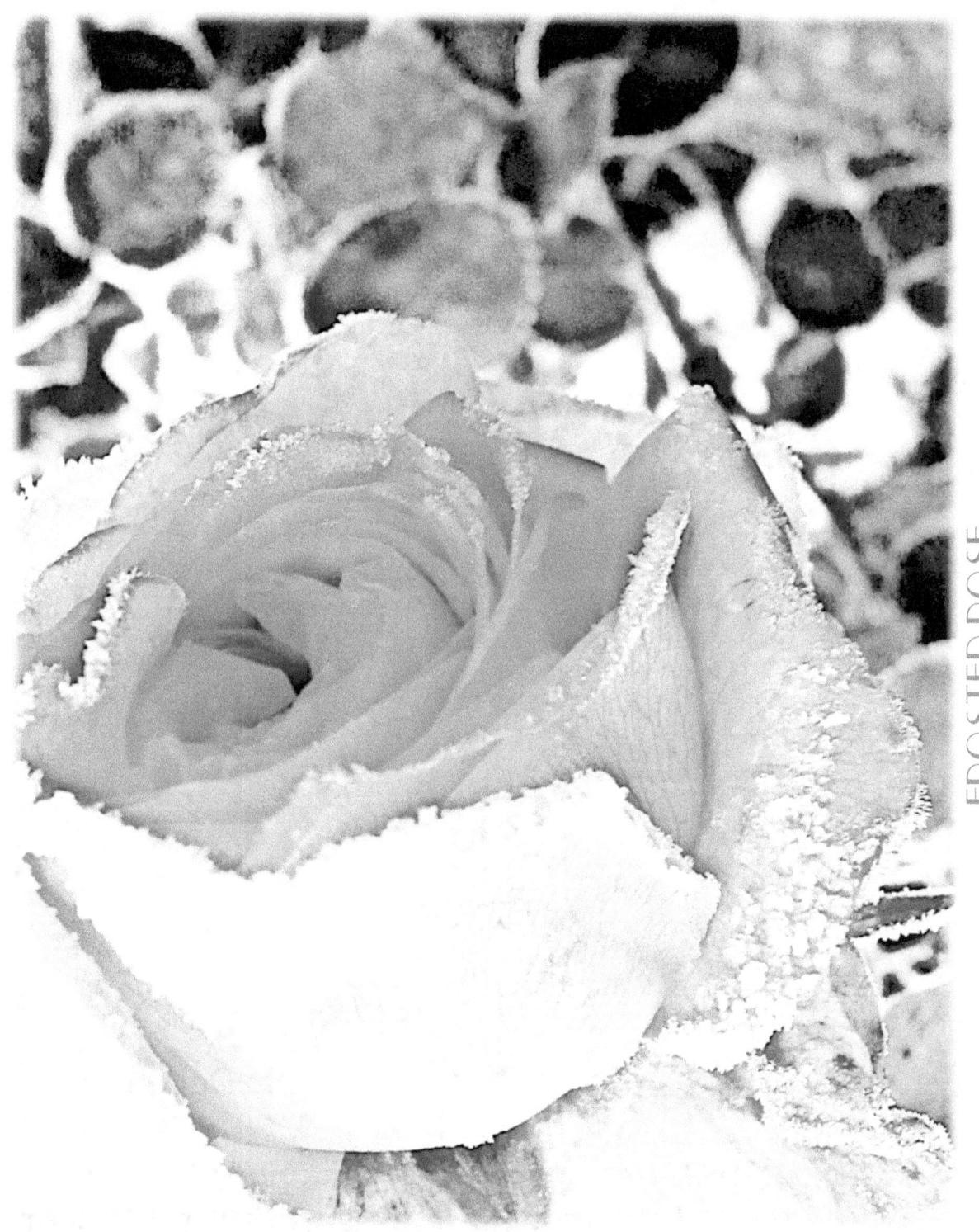

FROSTED ROSE

FROSTED ROSE I took this photo in December
ABRAHAM DARBY in Winter
AMAZON AUTHOR PAGE: www.amazon.com/author/janetlong
ETSY SHOP, "JLA" www.janetlongarts/shop/Etsy.com
ETSY VINTAGE SHOP: www.etsy.com/shop/AdoptionsLtd

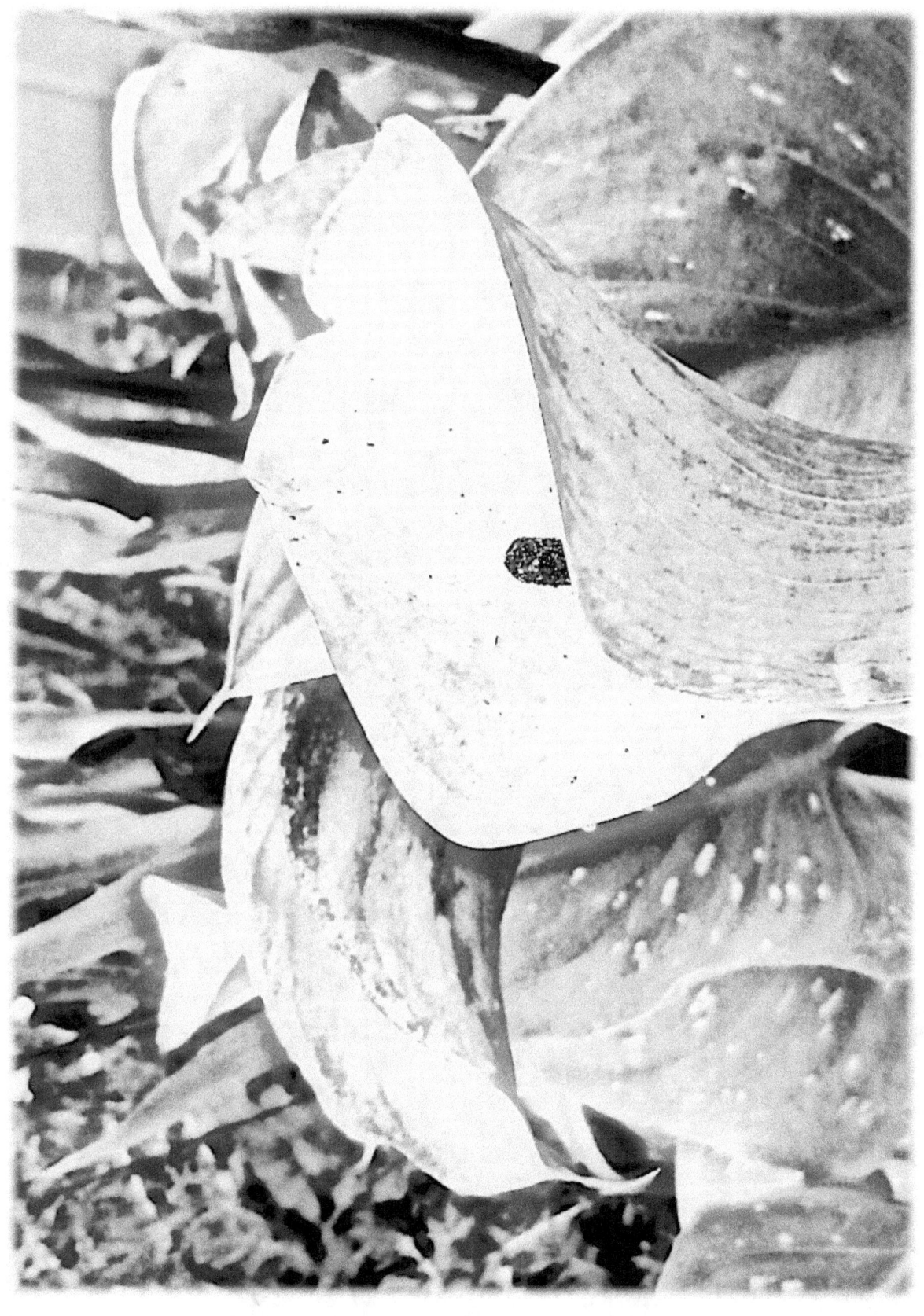

CALLA LILIES
AMAZON AUTHOR PAGE: www.amazon.com/author/janetlong
ETSY SHOP, "JLA" www.janetlongarts/shop/Etsy.com
ETSY VINTAGE SHOP: www.etsy.com/shop/AdoptionsLtd

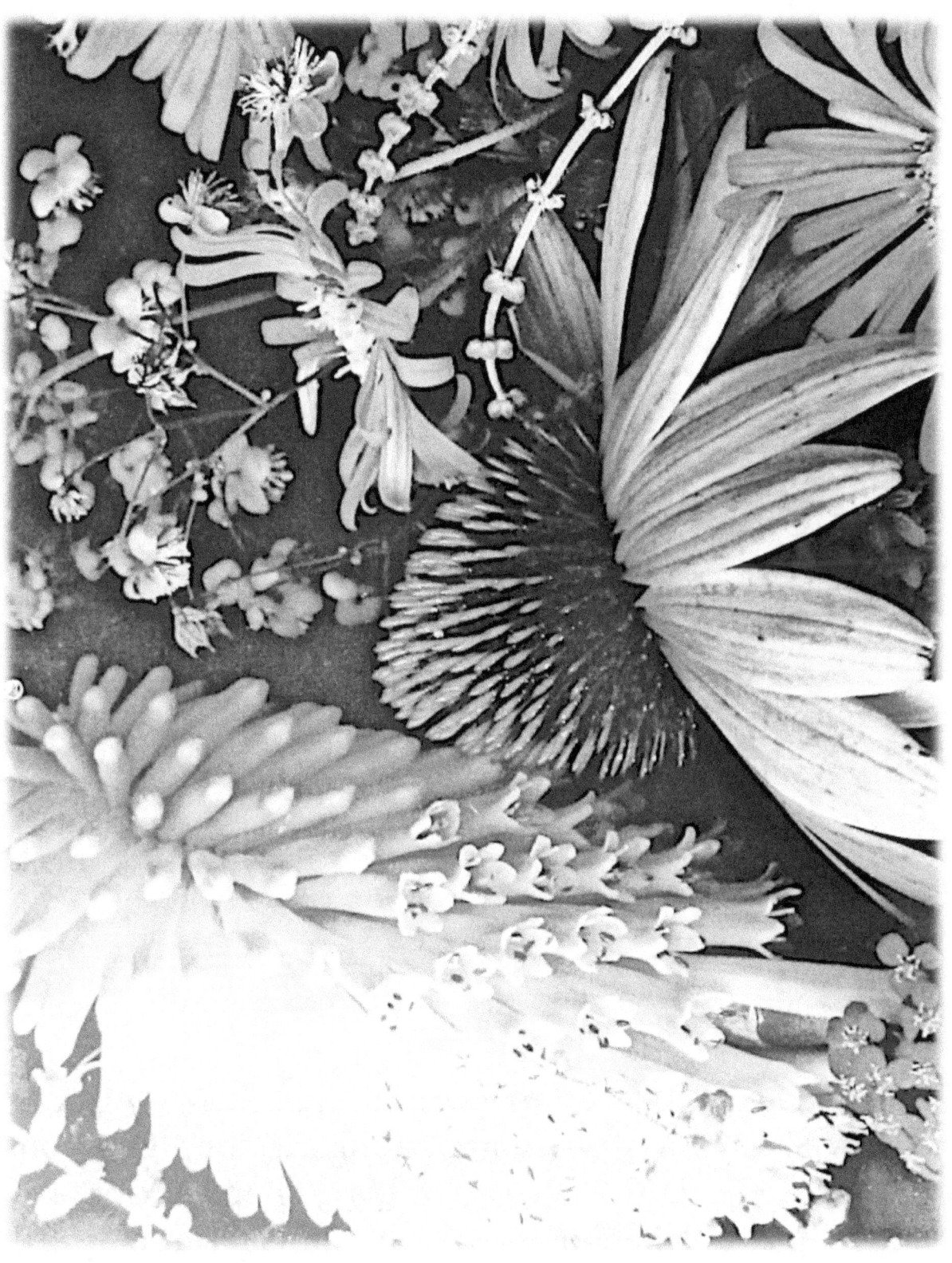

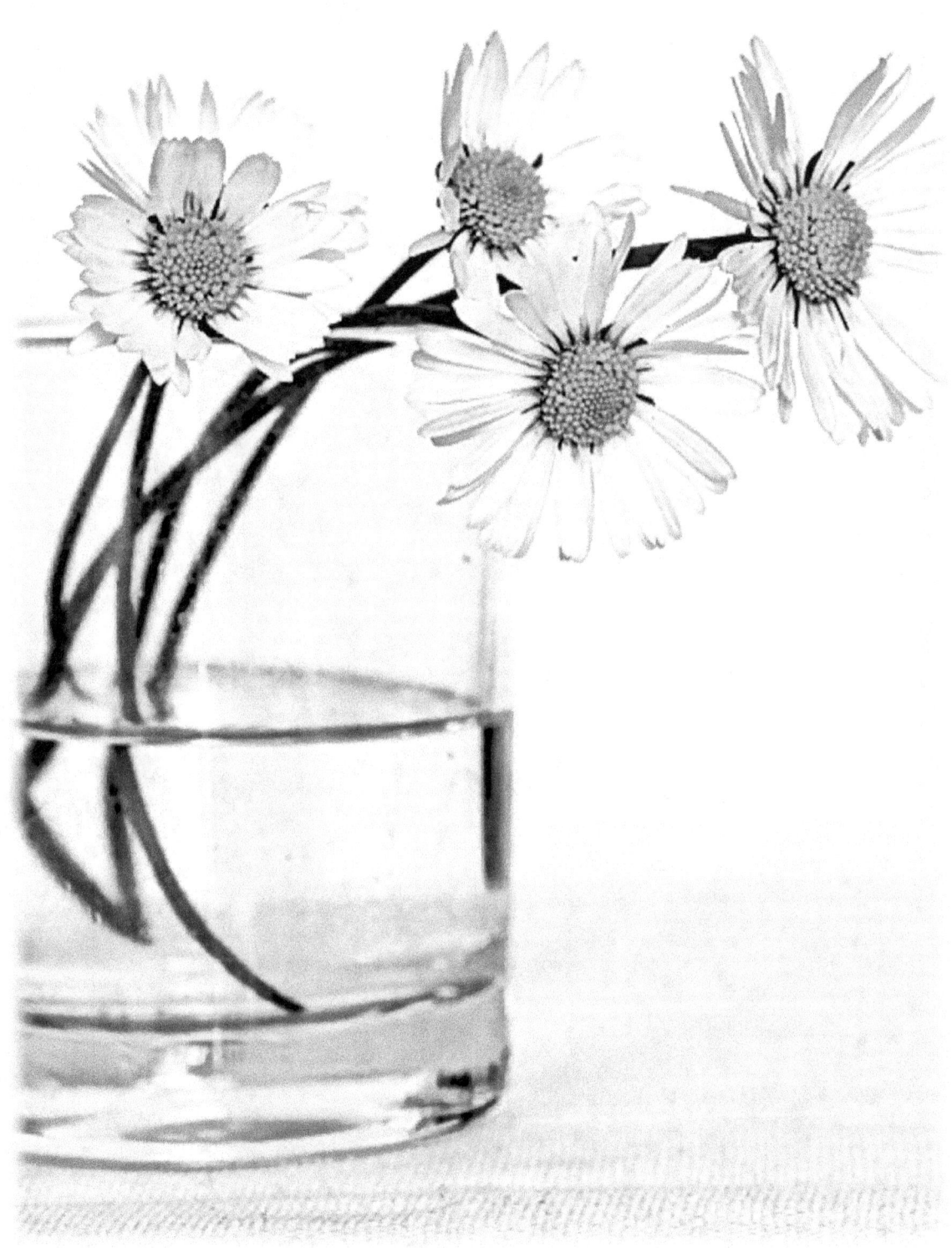

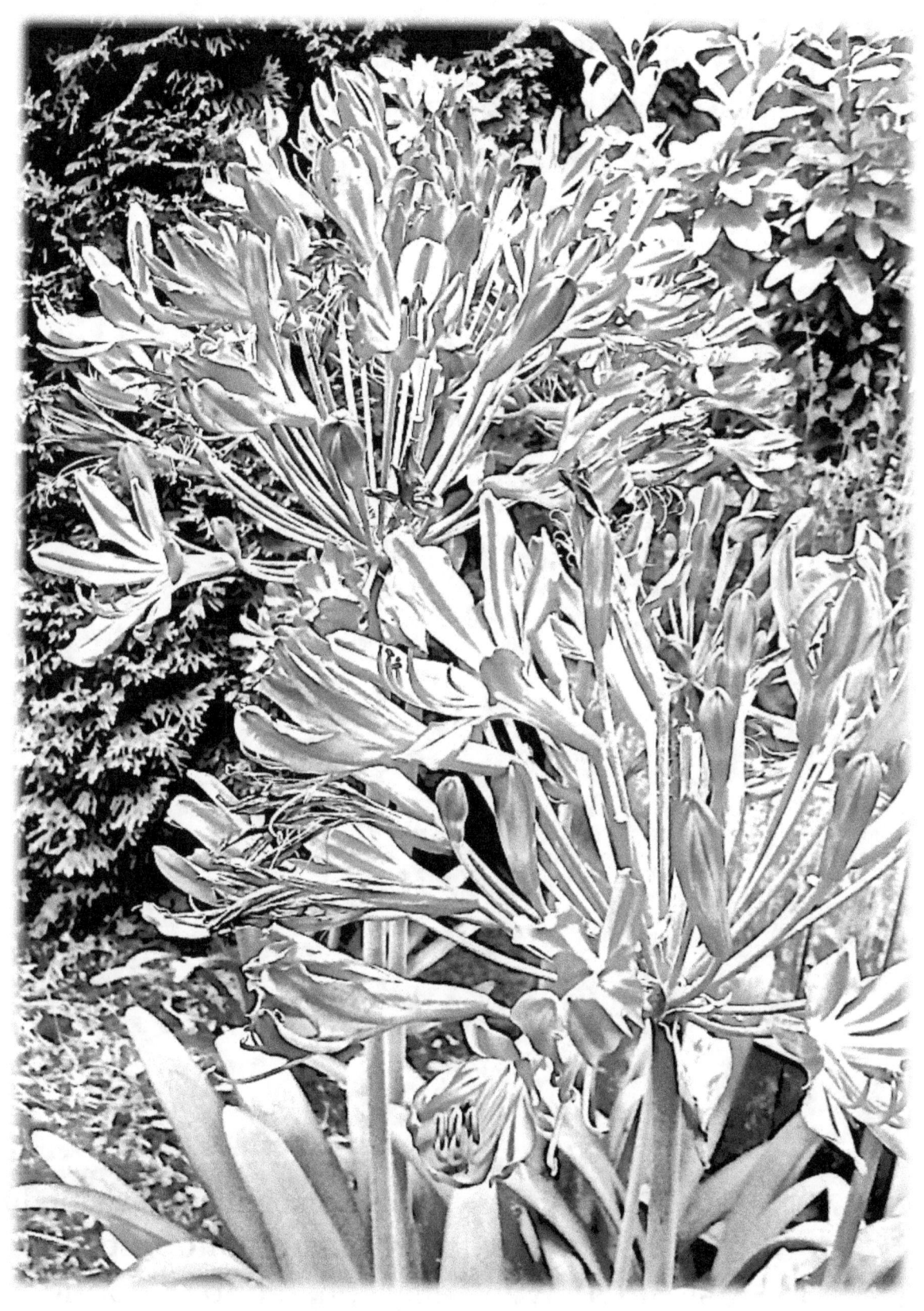

AGAPANTHUS

AGAPANTHUS
AMAZON AUTHOR PAGE: www.amazon.com/author/janetlong
ETSY SHOP, "JLA" www.janetlongarts/shop/Etsy.com
ETSY VINTAGE SHOP: www.etsy.com/shop/ AdoptionsLtd

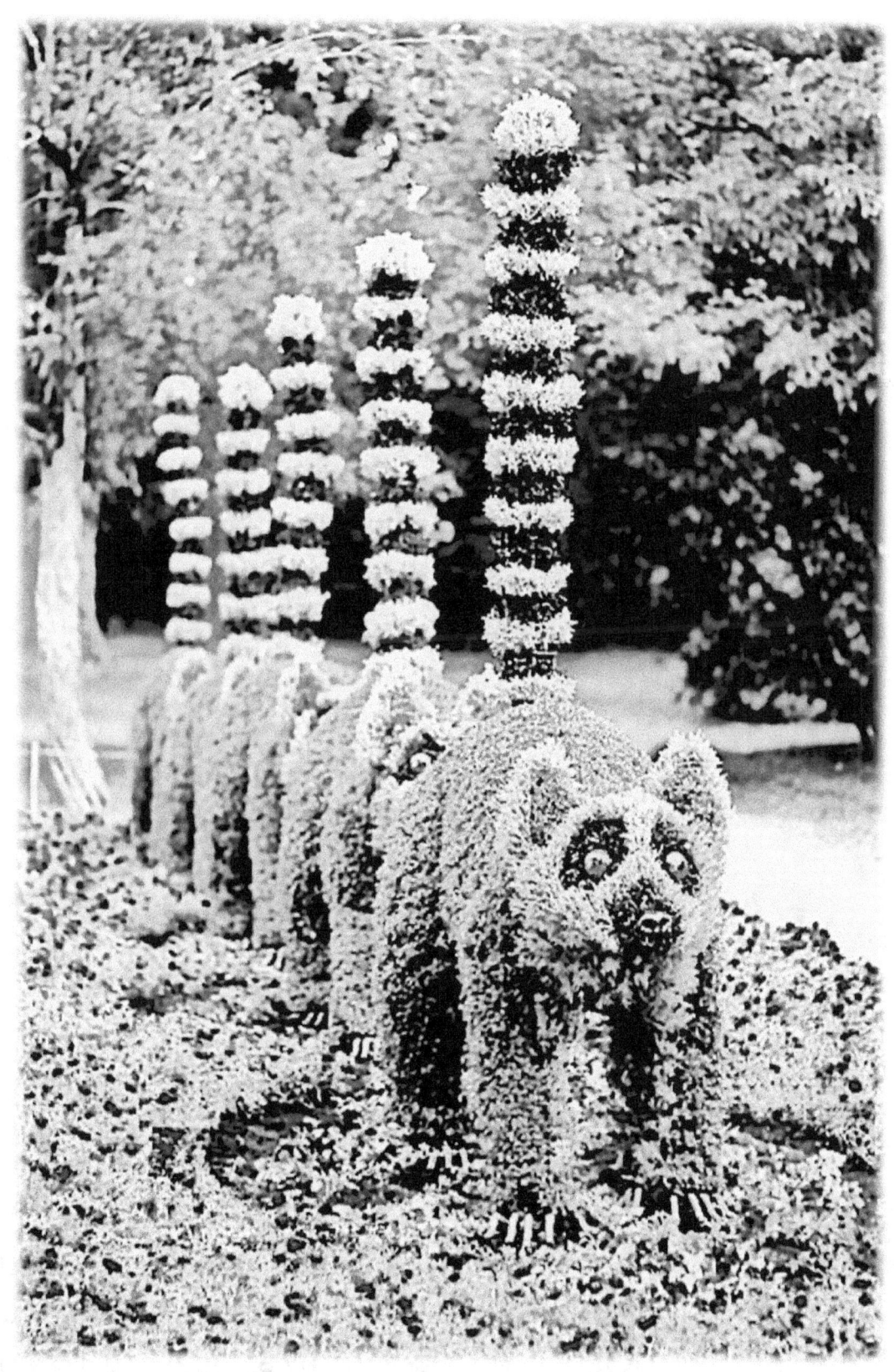

LEMUR LINE TOPIARY

LEMUR LINE TOPIARY
AMAZON AUTHOR PAGE: www.amazon.com/author/janetlong
ETSY SHOP, "JLA" www.janetlongarts/shop/Etsy.com
ETSY VINTAGE SHOP: www.etsy.com/shop/AdoptionsLtd

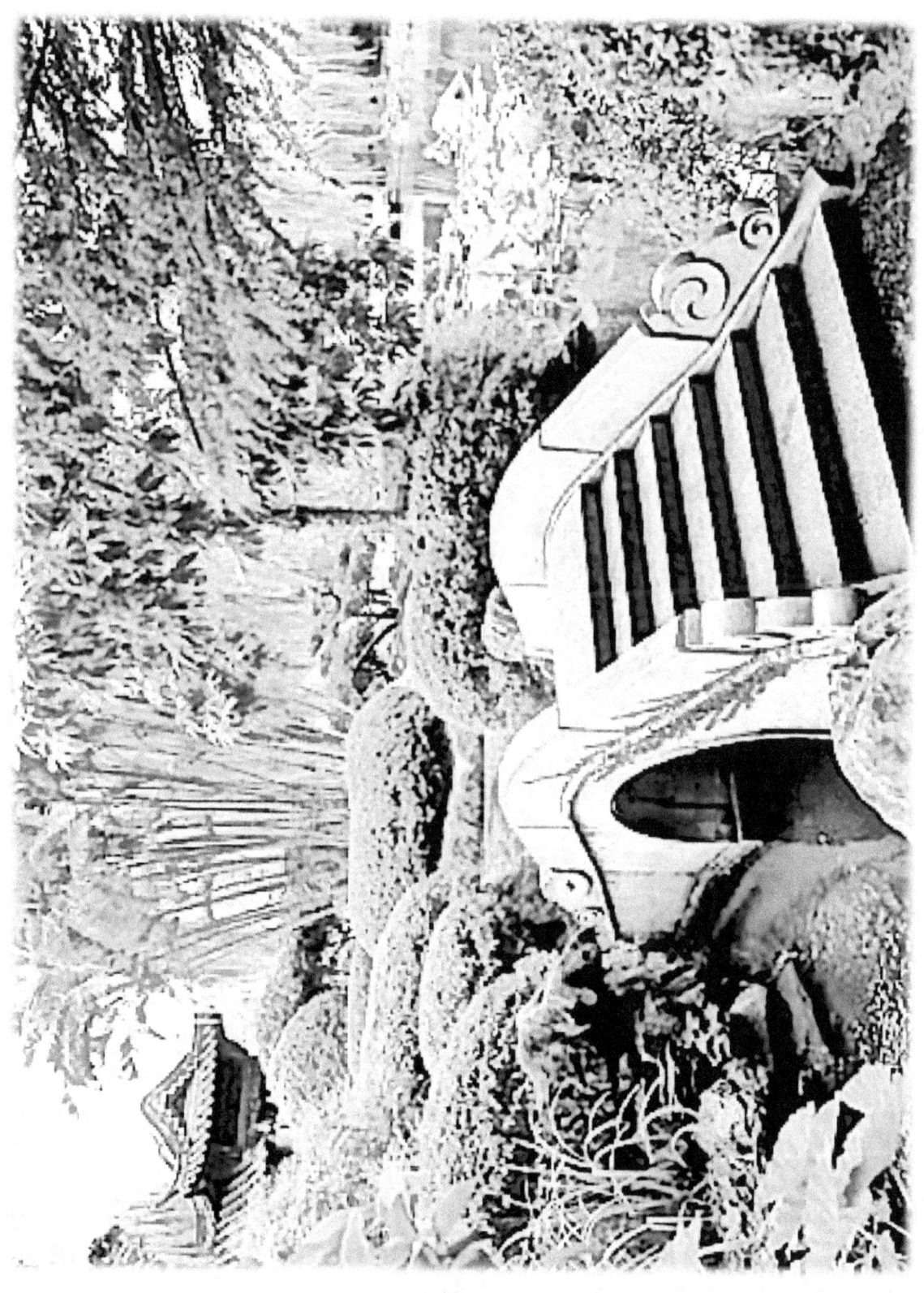

CHINESE GARDEN
AMAZON AUTHOR PAGE: www.amazon.com/author/janetlong
ETSY SHOP, "JLA" www.janetlongarts/shop/Etsy.com
ETSY VINTAGE SHOP: www.etsy.com/shop/ AdoptionsLtd

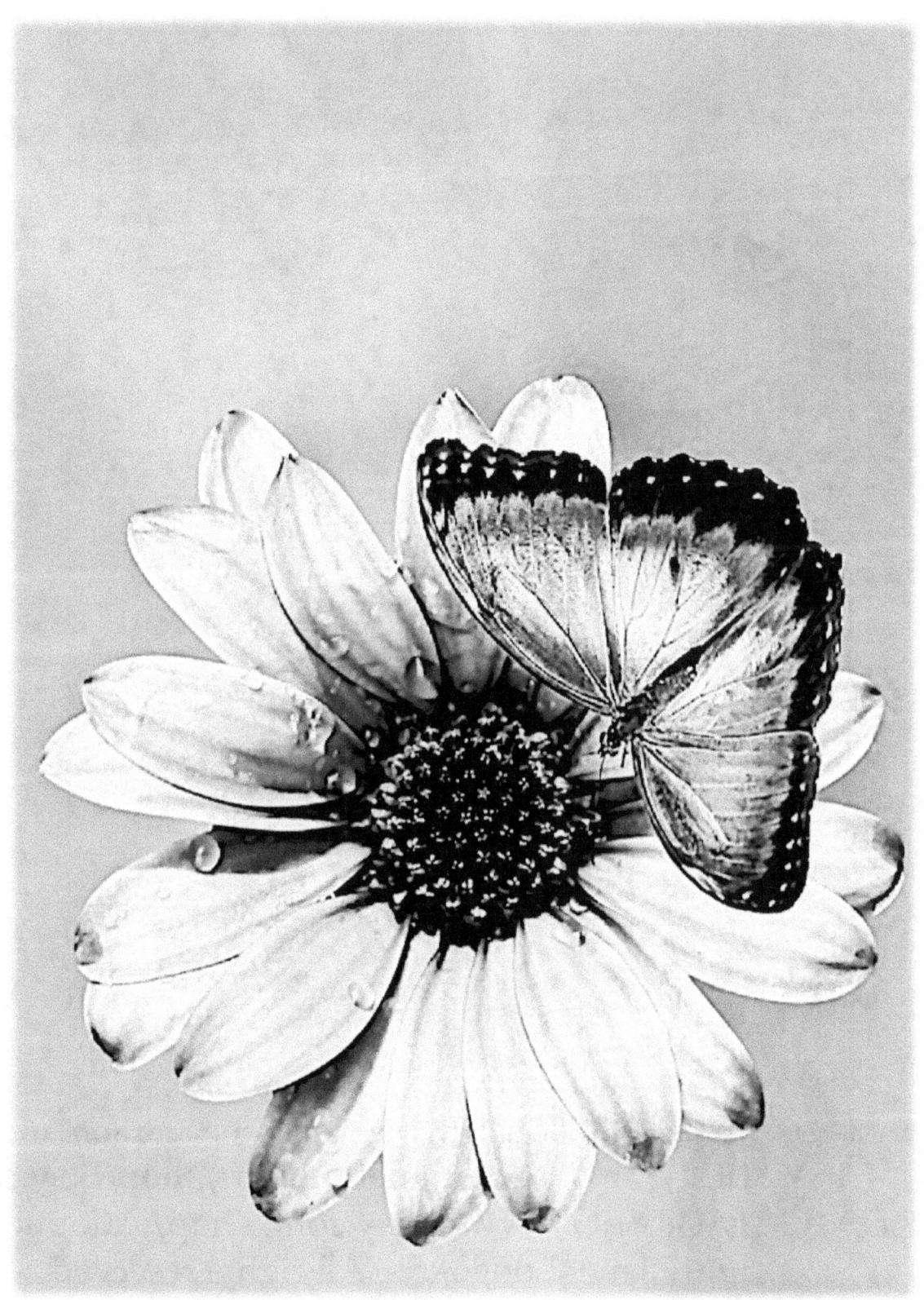

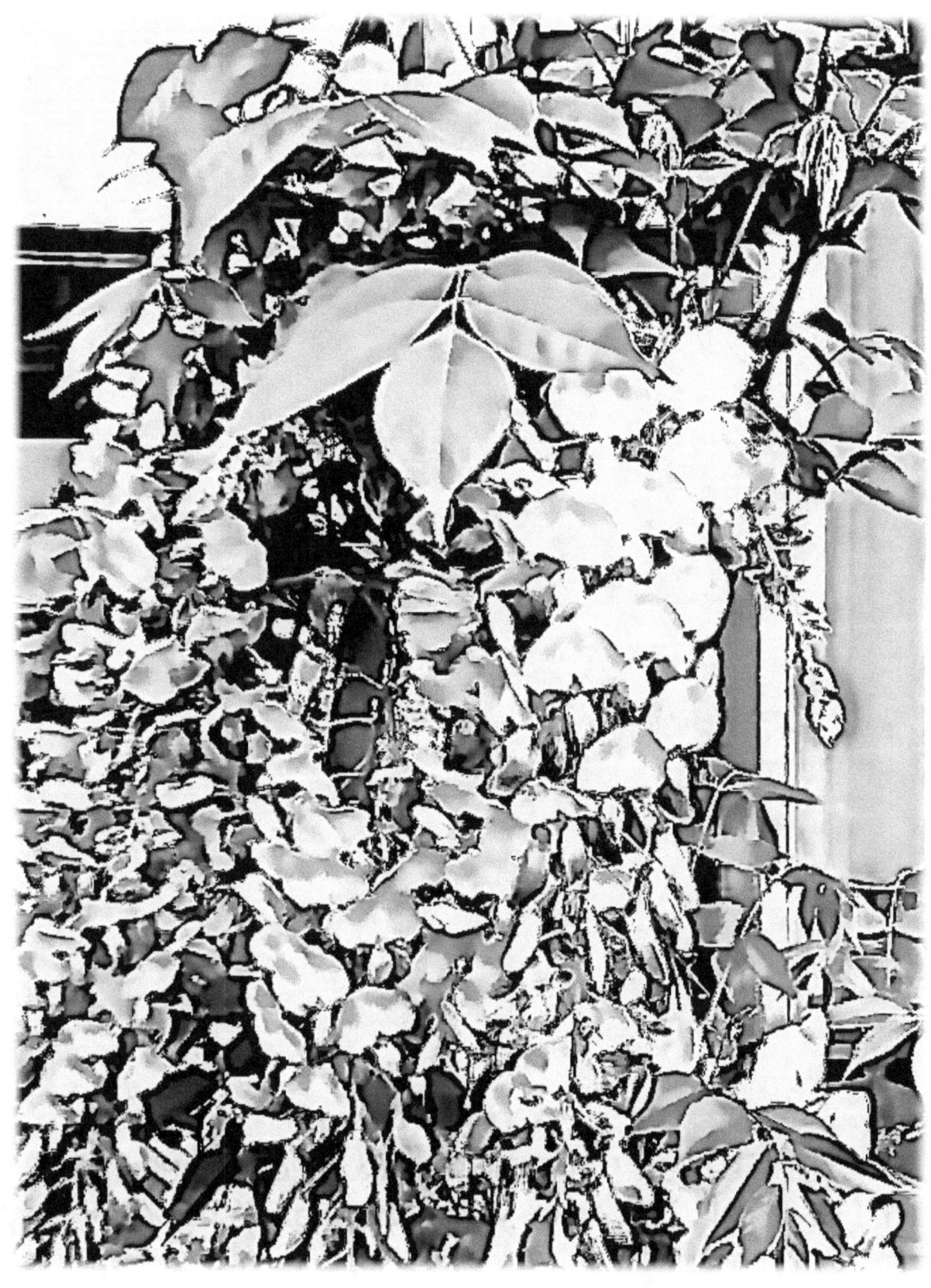

WISTERIA "BILL"

WISTERIA "BILL"
AMAZON AUTHOR PAGE: www.amazon.com/author/janetlong
ETSY SHOP, "JLA" www.janetlongarts/shop/Etsy.com
ETSY VINTAGE SHOP: www.etsy.com/shop/AdoptionsLtd

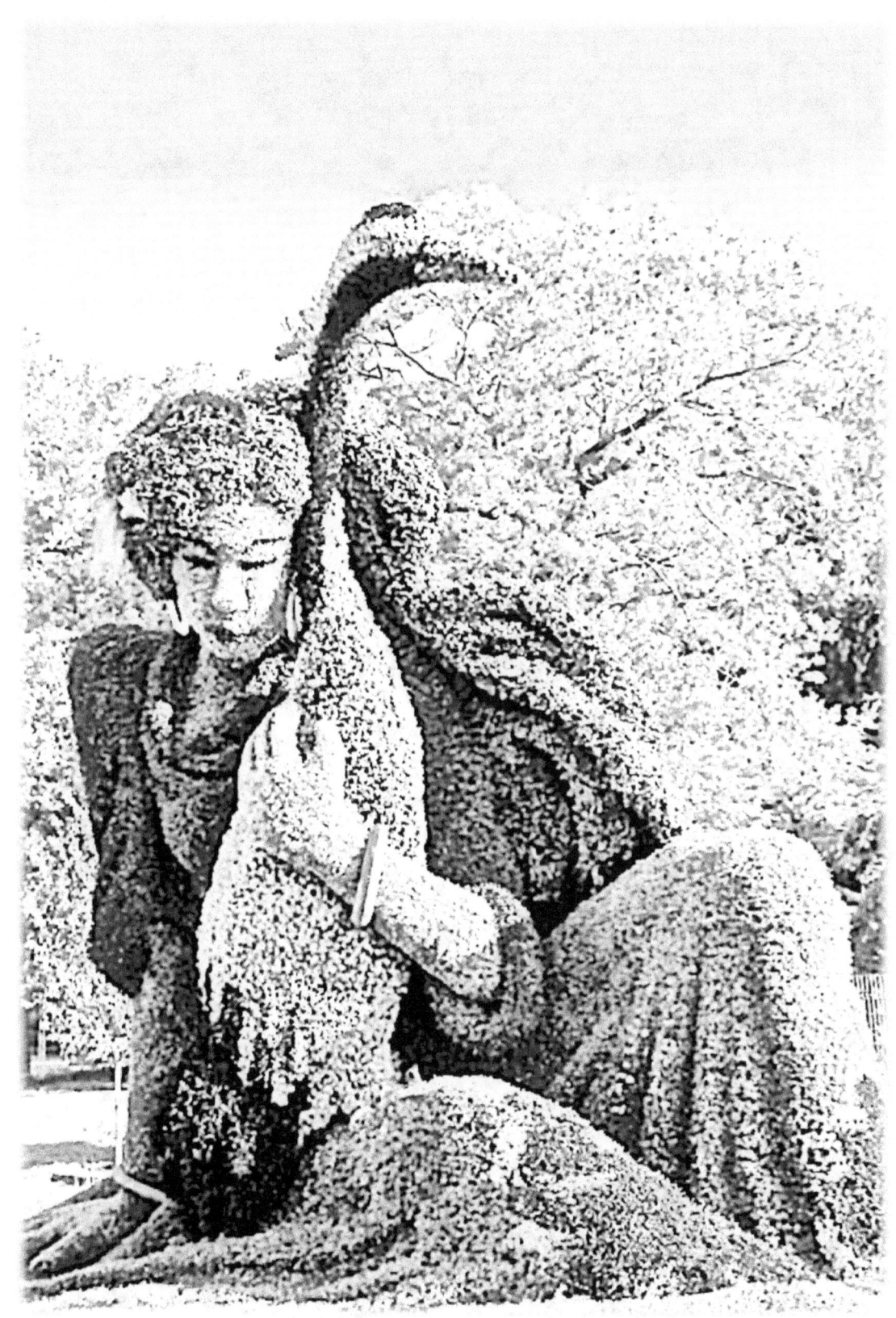

TOPIARY "MOTHER GOOSE"

TOPIARY "MOTHER GOOSE"
AMAZON AUTHOR PAGE: www.amazon.com/author/janetlong
ETSY SHOP, "JLA" www.janetlongarts/shop/Etsy.com
ETSY VINTAGE SHOP: www.etsy.com/shop/AdoptionsLtd

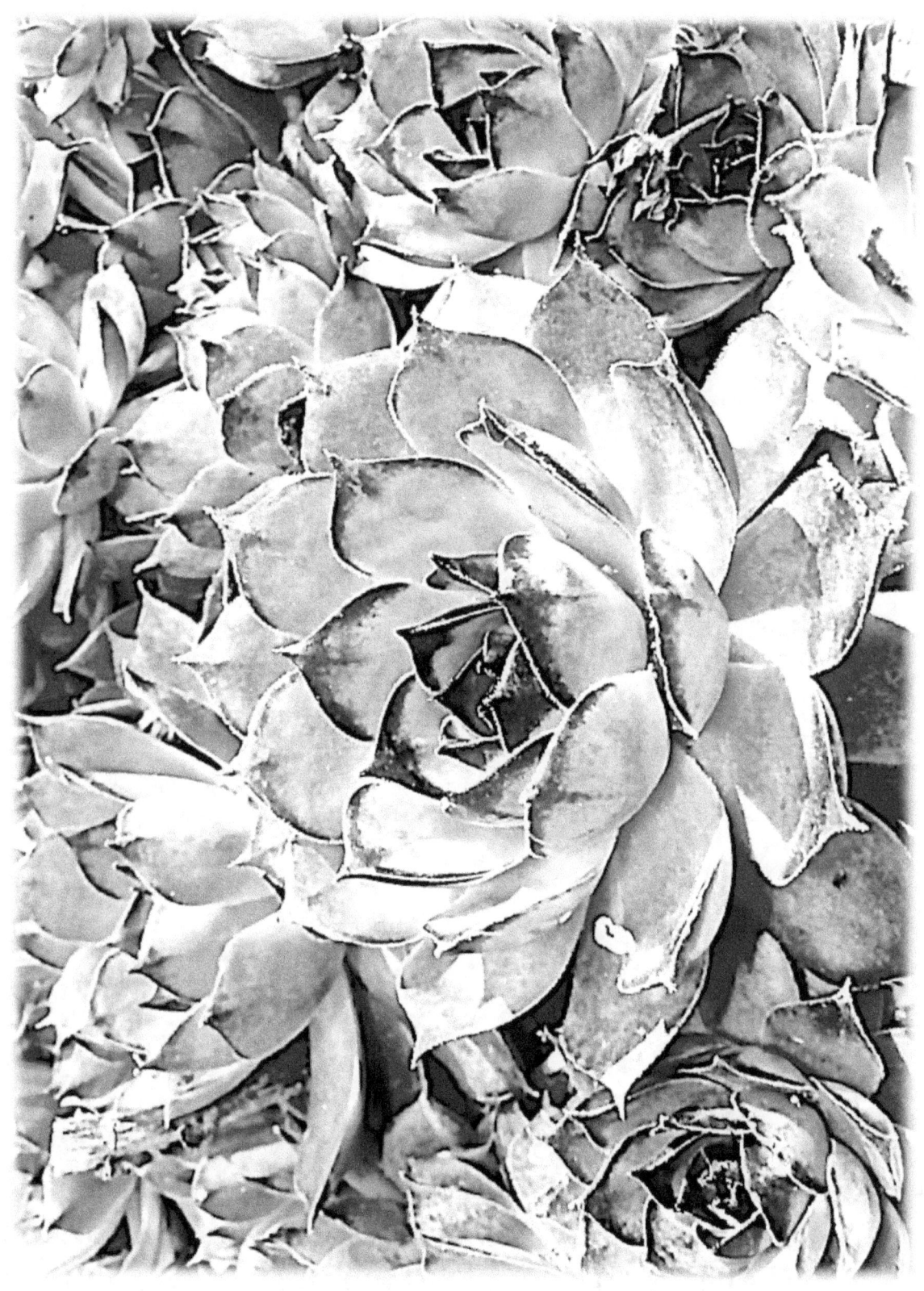

SUCCULENT

SUCCLENT
AMAZON AUTHOR PAGE: www.amazon.com/author/janetlong
ETSY SHOP, "JLA" www.janetlongarts/shop/Etsy.com
ETSY VINTAGE SHOP: www.etsy.com/shop/AdoptionsLtd

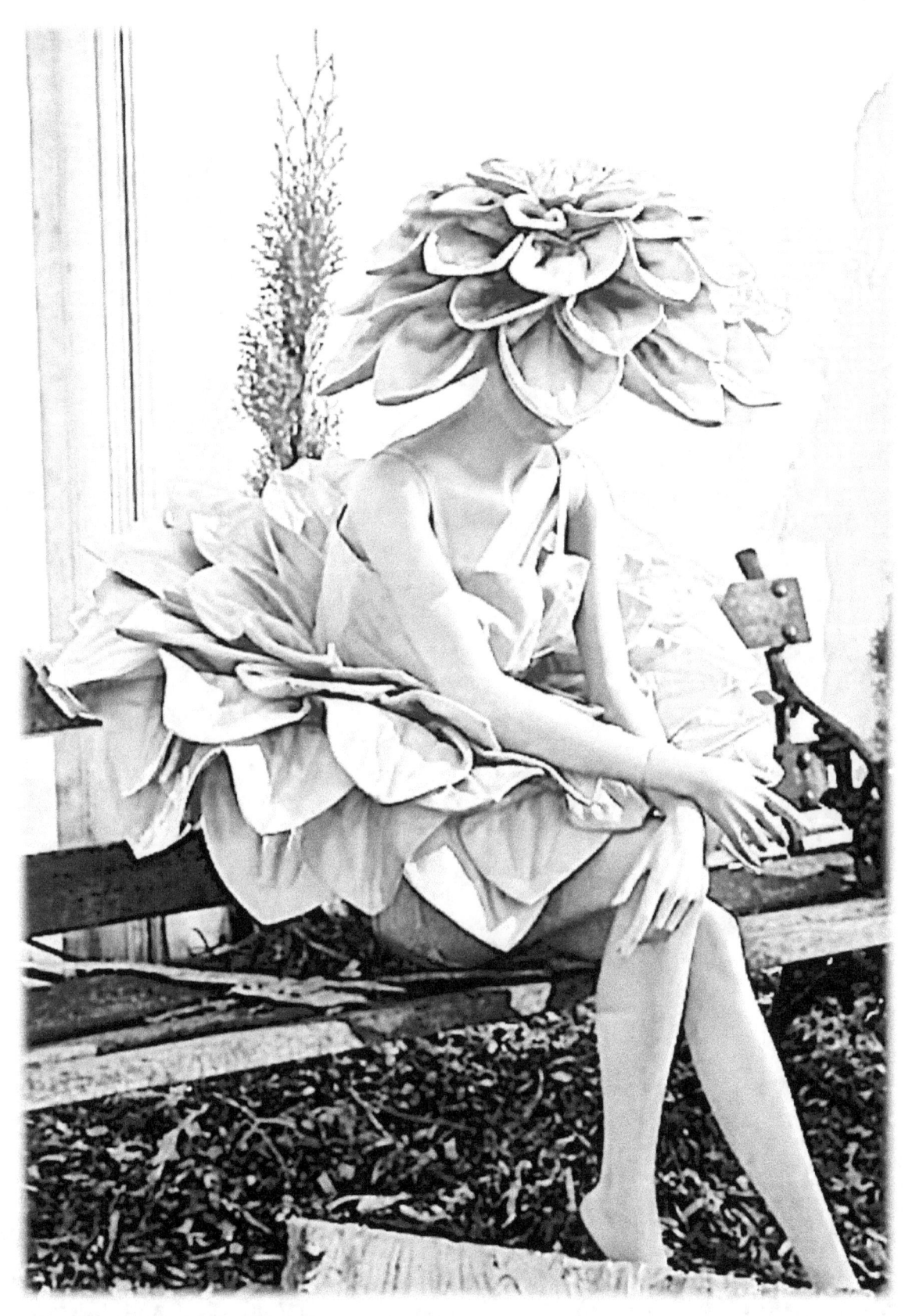

FLOWER COSTUME

FLOWER COSTUME
AMAZON AUTHOR PAGE: www.amazon.com/author/janetlong
ETSY SHOP, "JLA" www.janetlongarts/shop/Etsy.com
ETSY VINTAGE SHOP: www.etsy.com/shop/AdoptionsLtd

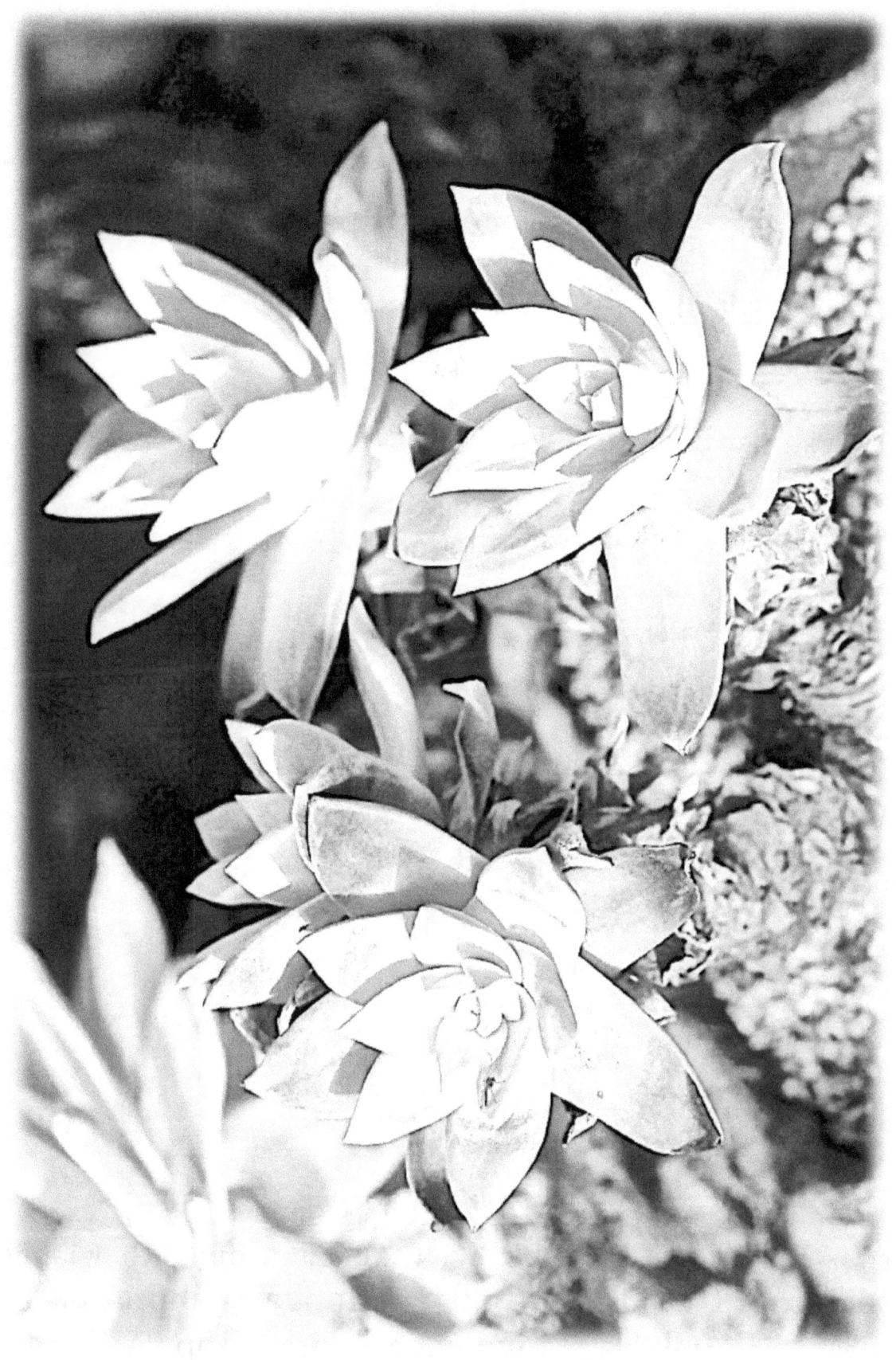

SUCCULENT

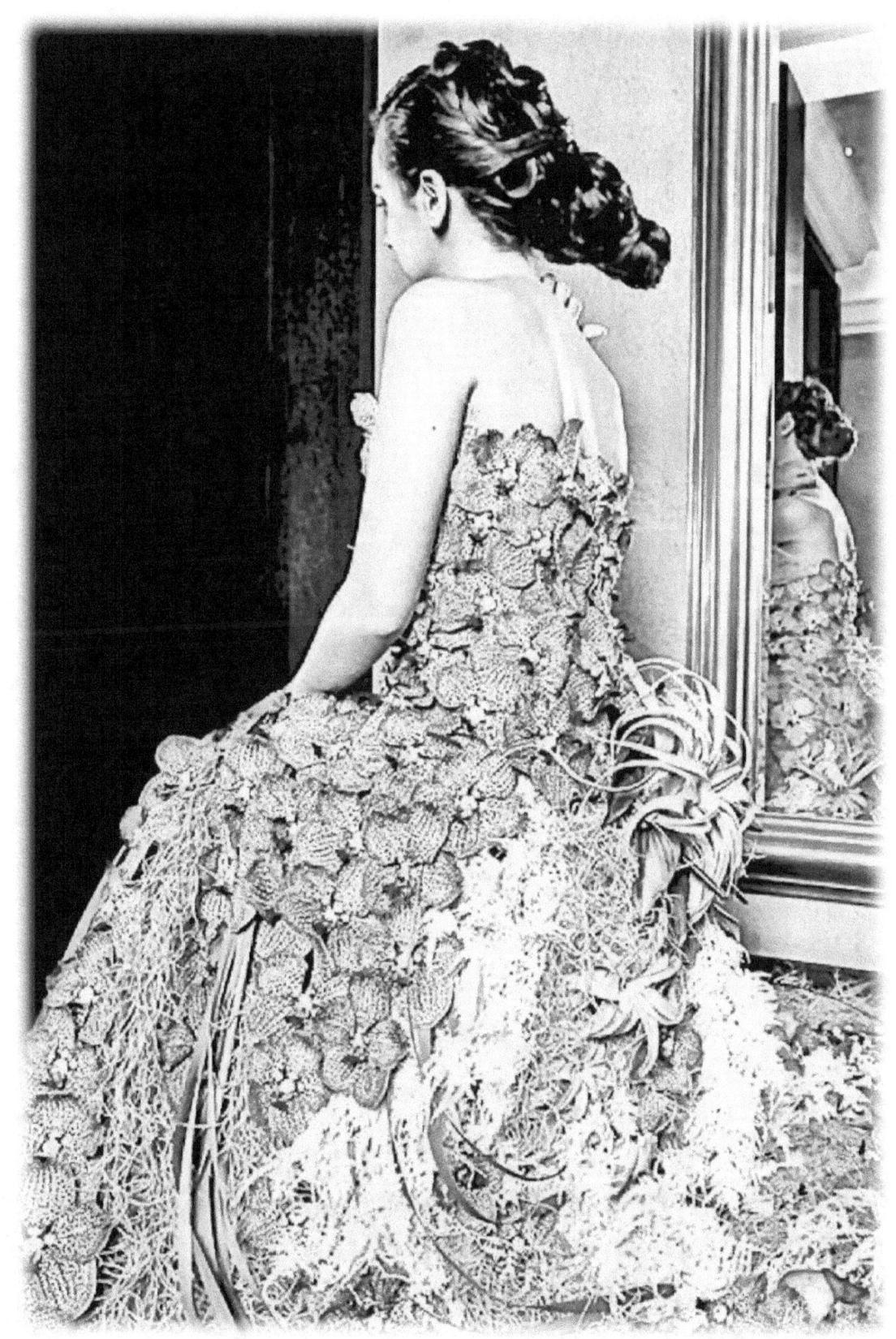

FLOWER GIRL DRESS?

FLOWER GIRL DRESS?
AMAZON AUTHOR PAGE: www.amazon.com/author/janetlong
ETSY SHOP, "JLA" www.janetlongarts/shop/Etsy.com
ETSY VINTAGE SHOP: www.etsy.com/shop/AdoptionsLtd

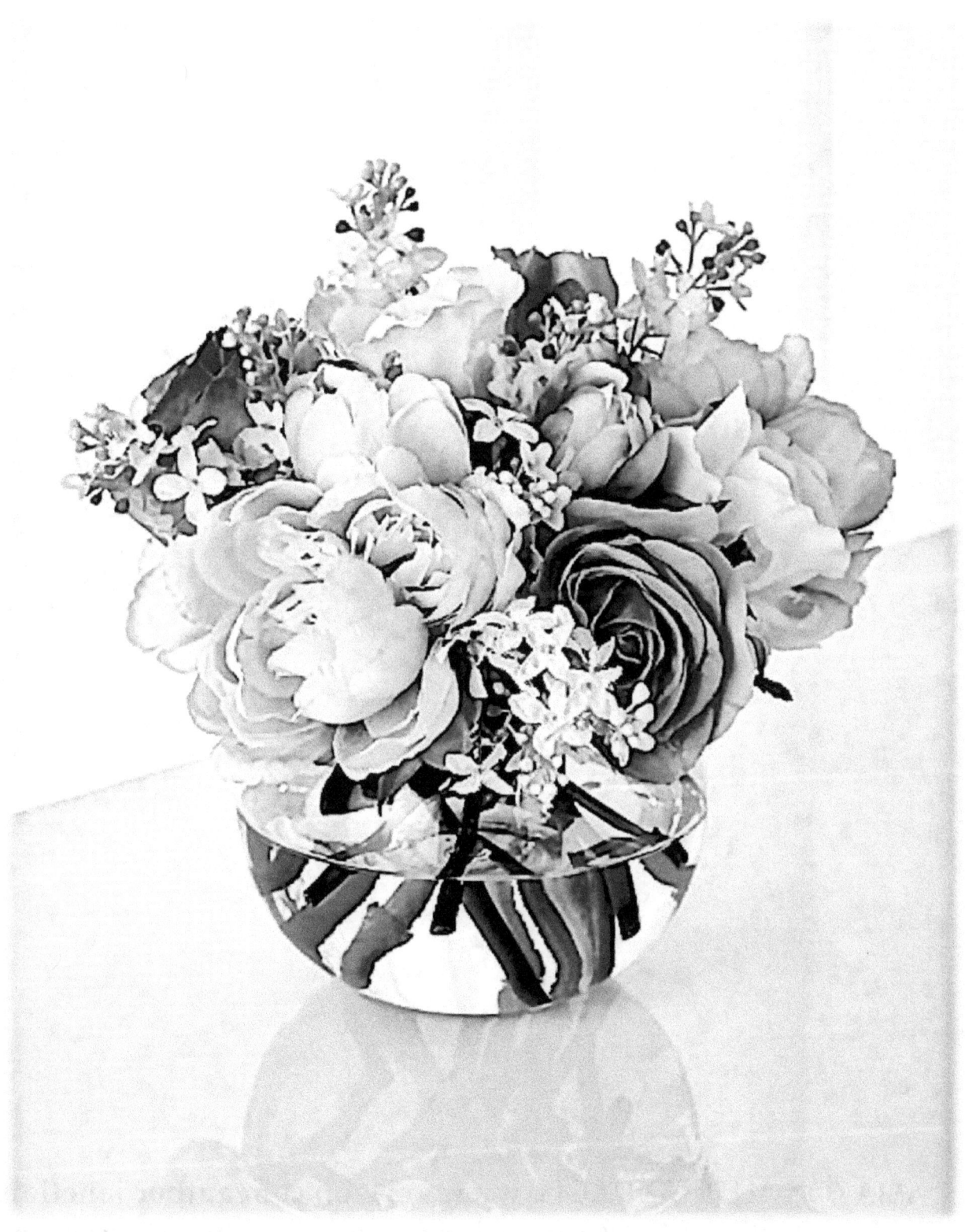

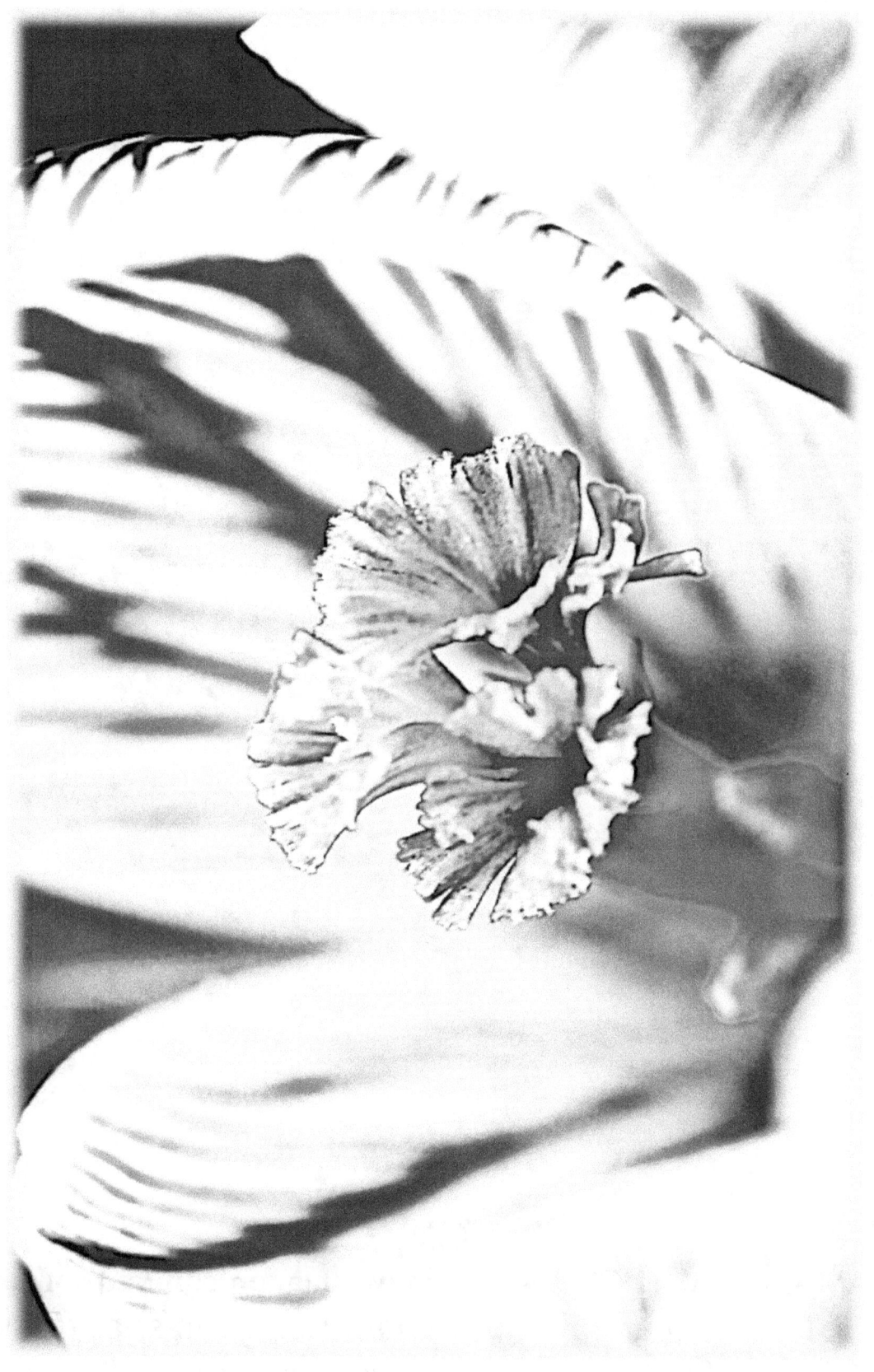

CROCUS
AMAZON AUTHOR PAGE: www.amazon.com/author/janetlong
ETSY SHOP, "JLA" www.janetlongarts/shop/Etsy.com
ETSY VINTAGE SHOP: www.etsy.com/shop/AdoptionsLtd

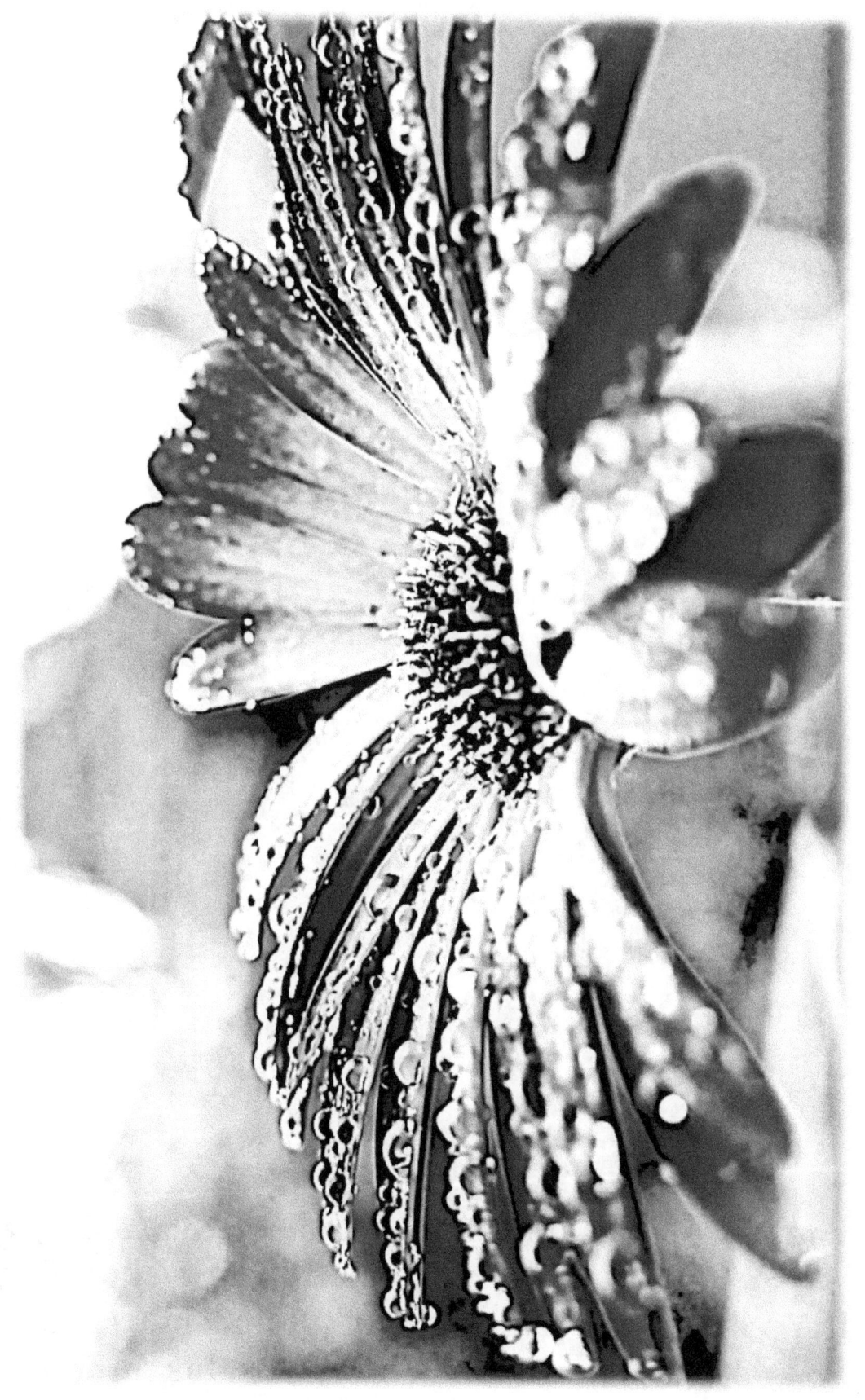

RAIN DROPS
AMAZON AUTHOR PAGE: www.amazon.com/author/janetlong
ETSY SHOP, "JLA" www.janetlongarts/shop/Etsy.com
ETSY VINTAGE SHOP: www.etsy.com/shop/AdoptionsLtd

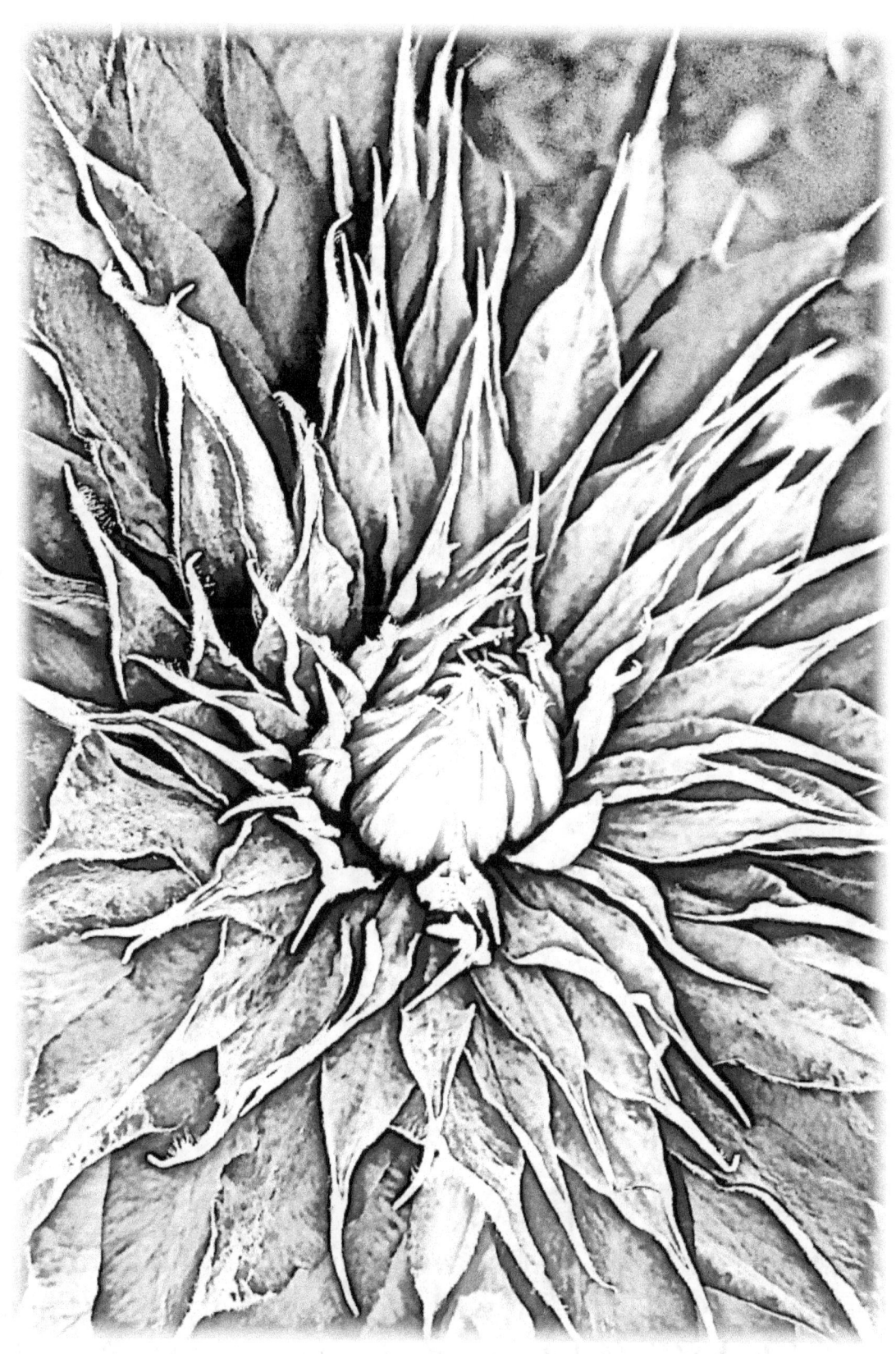

CLEMATIS "JOSEPHINE"

CLEMATIS "JOSEPHINE"
AMAZON AUTHOR PAGE: www.amazon.com/author/janetlong
ETSY SHOP, "JLA" www.janetlongarts/shop/Etsy.com
ETSY VINTAGE SHOP: www.etsy.com/shop/AdoptionsLtd

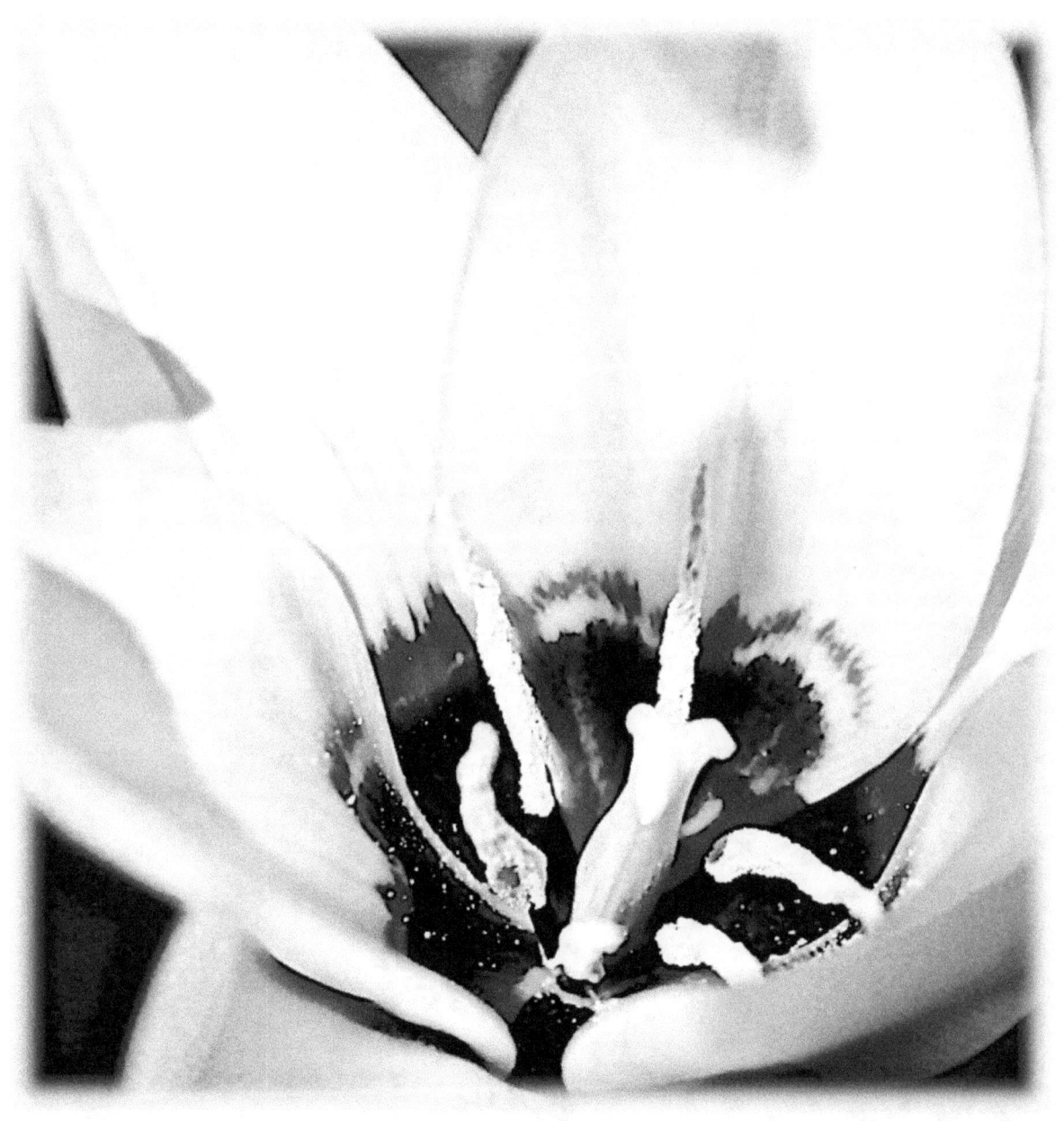

TULIP

TULIP
AMAZON AUTHOR PAGE: www.amazon.com/author/janetlong
ETSY SHOP, "JLA" www.janetlongarts/shop/Etsy.com
ETSY VINTAGE SHOP: www.etsy.com/shop/AdoptionsLtd

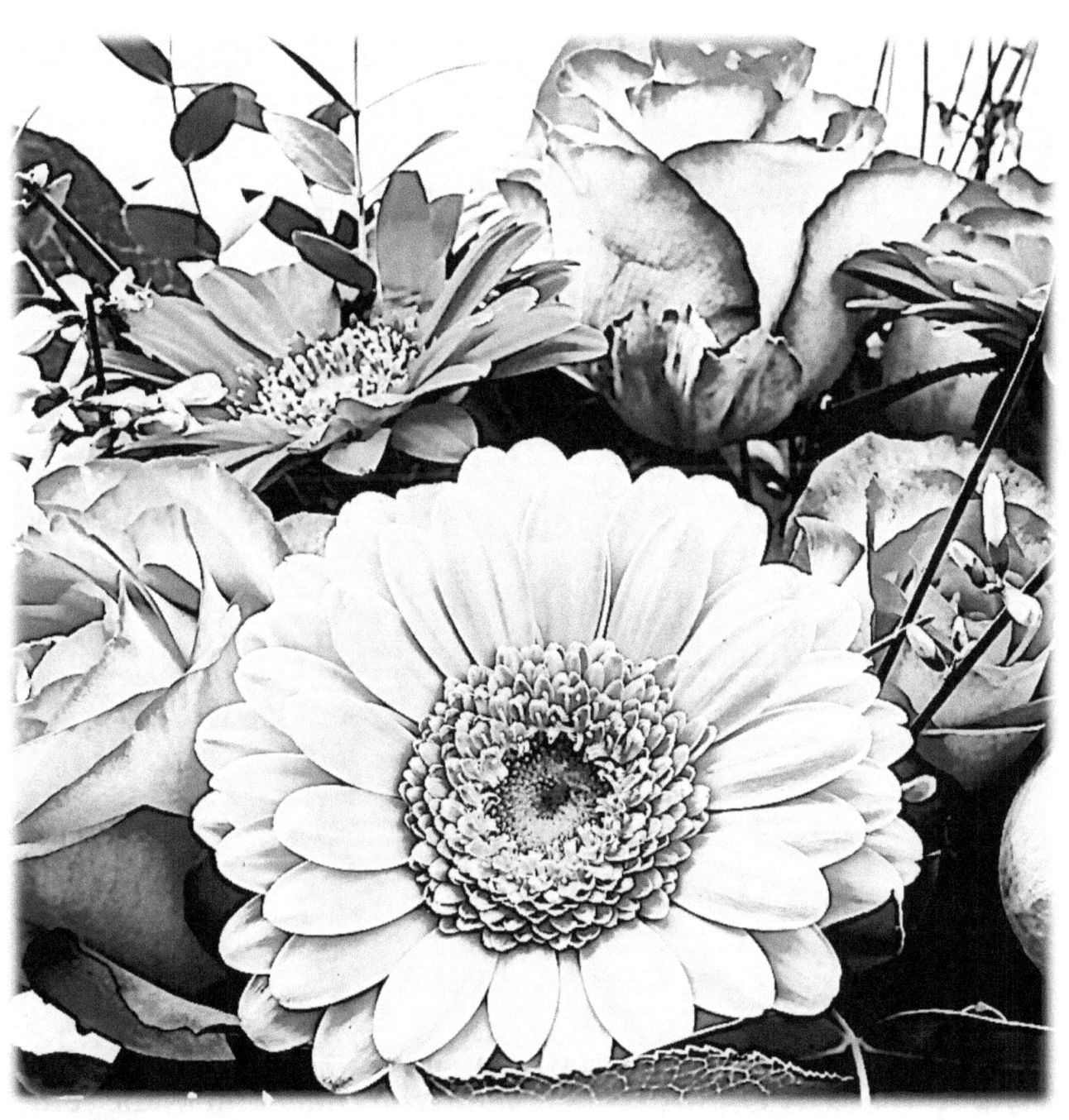

DAISIES & ROSES, OH MY!

DAISIES & ROSES, OH MY!
AMAZON AUTHOR PAGE: www.amazon.com/author/janetlong
ETSY SHOP, "JLA" www.janetlongarts/shop/Etsy.com
ETSY VINTAGE SHOP: www.etsy.com/shop/AdoptionsLtd

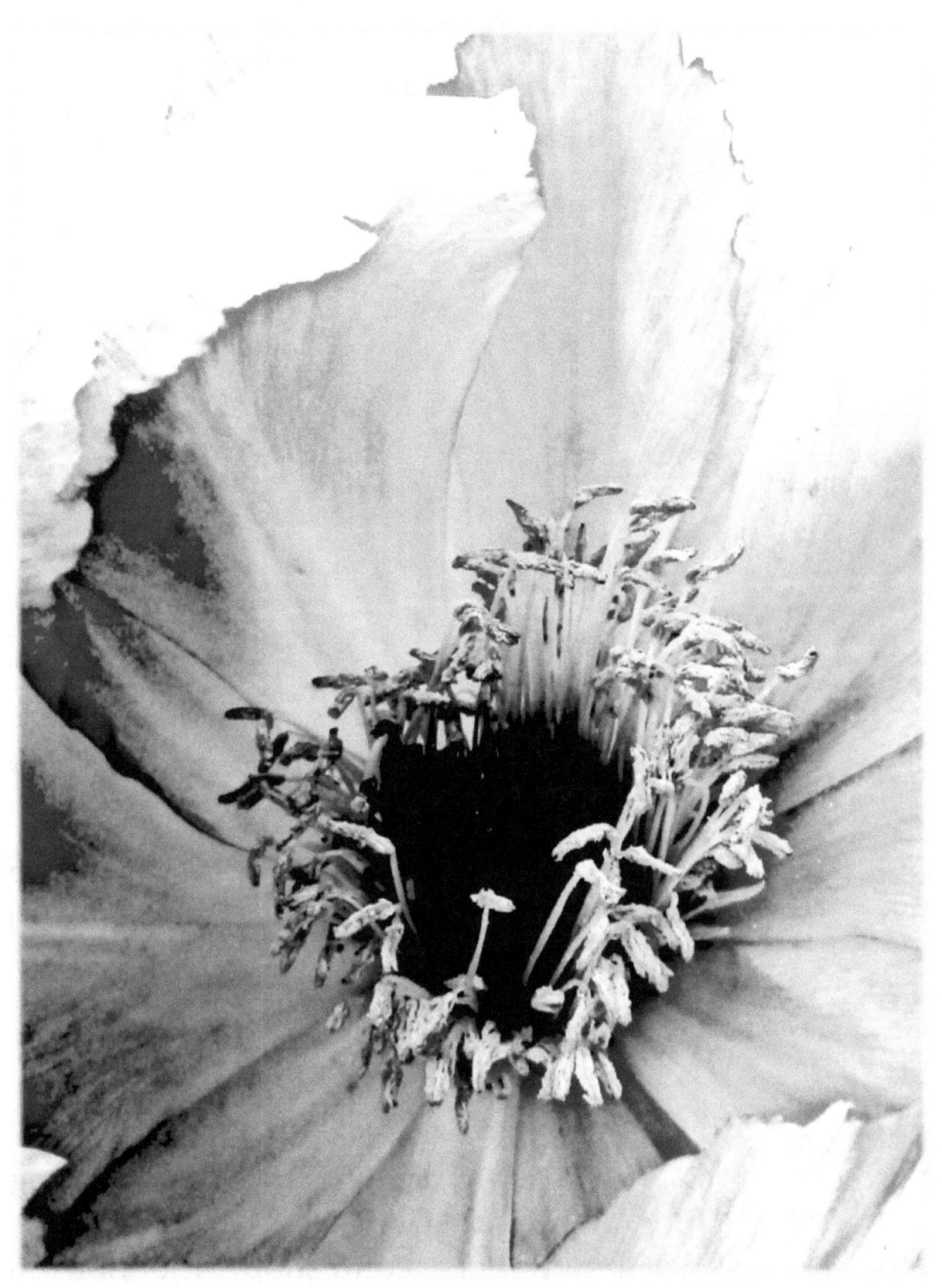

PEONY

PEONY
AMAZON AUTHOR PAGE: www.amazon.com/author/janetlong
ETSY SHOP, "JLA" www.janetlongarts/shop/Etsy.com
ETSY VINTAGE SHOP: www.etsy.com/shop/AdoptionsLtd

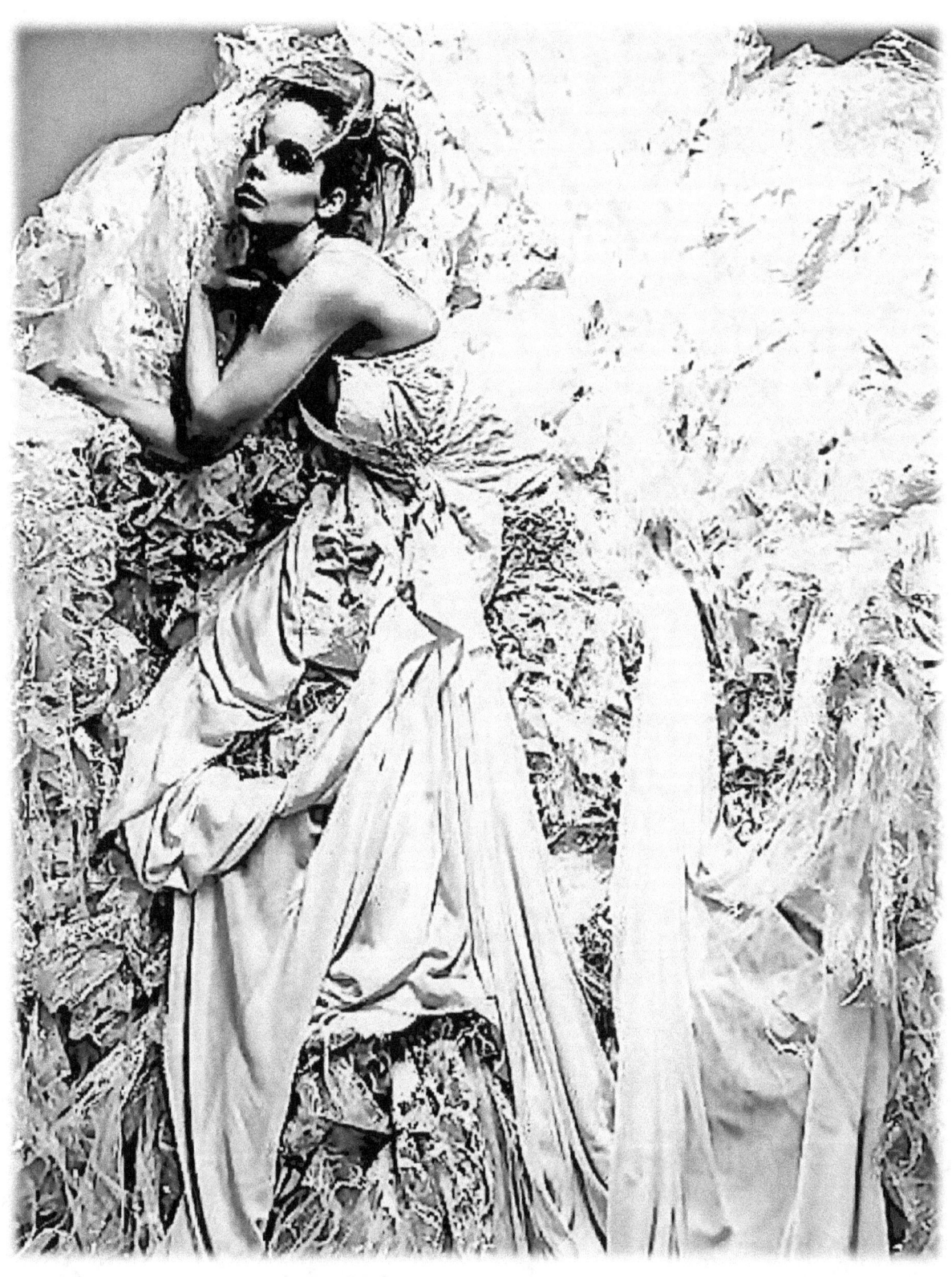

FLOWER DREAMS

FLOWER DREAMS
AMAZON AUTHOR PAGE: www.amazon.com/author/janetlong
ETSY SHOP, "JLA" www.janetlongarts/shop/Etsy.com
ETSY VINTAGE SHOP: www.etsy.com/shop/AdoptionsLtd

This page is for your notes & coloring tools tests

This page is for your notes & coloring tools tests

www.ingramcontent.com/pod-product-compliance
Lightning Source LLC
Chambersburg PA
CBHW081835170526
45167CB00007B/2817